The Long Island Indians and Their New England Ancestors

Narragansett, Mohegan, Pequot & Wampanoag Tribes

Donna Gentle Spirit Barron

Bloomington, IN

authorHOUSE™

Milton Keynes, UK

AuthorHouse™
1663 Liberty Drive, Suite 200
Bloomington, IN 47403
www.authorhouse.com
Phone: 1-800-839-8640

AuthorHouse™ UK Ltd.
500 Avebury Boulevard
Central Milton Keynes, MK9 2BE
www.authorhouse.co.uk
Phone: 08001974150

First published by AuthorHouse 6/16/2006

ISBN: 1-4259-3405-6 (sc)

Printed in the United States of America
Bloomington, Indiana

This book is printed on acid-free paper.

PREFIX

I, Princess Gentle Spirit have written this book not to proclaim anything other than what I am. For years I have been found to prove my heritage. This brings me to this stage of my life, where I want to share my research & family history with others.

Information obtained through out the years is factual. From MANY sources I have received documentation. I only write this book to inform those which denied me, who I am and the truth of my ancestors.

Any questions, comments, queries are well appreciated; however I have included citations of sources from References, Bibliographies, Historian's books, Family Records and Newspapers Articles and Oral Family Stories.

Growing up I was told that I am Native American on my Father's side and that we are related to the "Thirteen Tribes of Long Island". But like most children, I did not take much interest because my Elder's said "We do not speak of it, for it is not proper".

As years have gone by, not much thought was given to my heritage. I grew up in the small Town of Flushing, with my family and friends.

In 1996 I decided to find out about my heritage. Through revelations of my life and with assistance of friends, I started to look for answers to the questions and curiosity that I had.

Some questions were: "Who my Grandparents were"? "Where did they come from"? "What Tribes were they from, exactly"? And "What were their lives like"?

As I am sure many people have the same questions about their own family.

I became tired of wondering and wanted answers. I found an old copy of an incomplete family tree that a distant relative had given my Father and I started from there.

The information in this tree, gave me a starting point. I have contacted family members, to see how they could help me.

Answers I received from many had been the same. Everyone used a similar copy of the family tree, my Father had given me. This did not answer my questions. I became determined to know, learn of the truth, I sought.

Some of whom I asked, were eager to assist me at first, as they did not know who I was. To them, I was just a name on paper. As I have learned through the years, sharing a family story is sacred. Which is why some of these stories will not be included in this book.

It is thanks to them, I have fought, searched and dug and I have come out with such great knowledge.

Knowledge to which can be shared and those family secrets that cannot.

The information I have dates back to my seventeenth Great Grandfather, the birth of Sachem Weeroum.

This is where I shall begin my ancestral line.

I hope you enjoy reading and learning, as much as I did.

From this point forward, I will be speaking of the Thirteen Tribes of Long Island and their: Narragansett, Wampanoag, Mohegan and Pequot ancestors and how they are my family.

DEDICATION:

I dedicate this book to the memory of my Great, Great Grand Uncle. "Known by" Chief John Standing Waters and to his Grandson, whom I am proud to call cousin, LaRocque Mongotucksee Waters.

For without them, my interest in my heritage would not have been. The knowledge gained would never have been obtained. I love you. God Bless.

Thank you to my son, Eric, for his writings inspire me. Thank you for all your help and the beautiful cover! And to Gerald T. Hylla, you're AMAZING!!!! Thank you!

"We are not an extinct Race, but alive and full of fight for a restoration of our rights and privileges".

Chief John H. Standing Waters

"The Pilgrims were not simple refugees from England fighting against oppression and religious discrimination. They were Political Revolutionaries and part of the Puritan movement considered objectionable and unorthodox by the King of the Church of England. Outcasts and fugitives in their own homeland, they plotted to take over the government. When unsuccessful, they had to relocate or face prosecution. After several attempts at finding a suitable new home, they elected to try their luck in the New World. Here they thought they could build their own promised land"...............

Terri Jean
"The National Day of Mourning"
A Different Thanksgiving Perspective.

TABLE OF CONTENTS

CHAPTER ONE
"Narragansett Indian"

The Narragansett Indian Tribe was once a most powerful federation. Once referred as "Narrowhansetts" and "Narigansets". Meaning: "People of the Small Point". They subsisted by hunting, fishing and partially by agriculture.

They would spend a great deal of their day in the fields tending to their corn crop which was their major staple. They also gathered nuts and berries and other plants. The Narragansetts would seasonally move to where food was readily available.

The typical family lived by the sea in summer, building wigwams of skins, mats, or bark, supported by poles. In the winter, they lived inland. Their winter home called a long house, housed up to twenty families which sheltered them over the cold winter months.

The Narragansett numbered twenty or twenty-five thousand, with a war strength of three to five thousand.

The tribe originally occupied most of the territory along the western shore of Narragansett Bay in Rhode Island, including the Niantic territory, from Providence River on the northeast to Pawcatuck River on the southwest.on the northwest they claimed control over a part of the country of the Coweset and Nipmuc, and on the southwest they claimed by conquest from the Pequot a strip extending to the Connecticut line.

The Narragansett claimed dominion over several small tribes of the interior and the neighboring islands, including Long Island.

They were a strong, generous and brave race. The Narragansett formed the second of the five great federations of New England Indians.

The tribe and its members were considered Warriors within their region and organized under powerful "Kings". They were made up of several sub- tribes and Chief, Sachems.

CHAPTER TWO
"Narragansett Sachem"
Weeroum

My ancestor, Weeroum, who was born in the year 1432, in Quinebaug, Mass. was a Chief Sachem of the Narragansett.

He married Kesh-ke-choo-watt-ka-Gunsh, she a Narragansett Indian in the year 1457.

They had three children together. Their son, Tashtassuck was the Chief, Sachem when the explorer Giovanni de Verrazno first visited the Narragansett Bays in 1524.

Tashtassuck was a vain Chief, and viewed himself and the Narragansett as a superior race over neighboring Indian Nations. He felt none had been his equal and found no one worthy, so he gave his daughter in marriage to his son, "Wessonsuium" Wessoum.

Narragansett traditional positions included a Sub-Chief, War Chief, Chief Scout, Tribal Medicine Man, a Historian and a Prophet.

The language of the Narragansett is of the Algonquin origin. They were an Eastern Woodland People. Not only were they good Hunters and Fishermen, they were expert users of water. The Narragansett were proficient swimmers as well as expert canoe men. They spent a great deal of time building and repairing their canoes which was their primary means of transportation.

The tribe and its members were considered Warriors within the region. The Narragansett customarily offered protection to smaller tribes in the area. Certain Nipmuck bands, the Niantics, Wampanoag and Manisseans all paid tribute to the Narragansett tribe.

They established themselves as the dominant tribe in Southern New England.

Chief, Sachem Tashassuck died about 1620. The succession to Chief authority was generally preserved in the family.

In the year 1621 Tashassuck's Great Grandson Canonicus inherited the Narragansett Sachem title role.

He ruled the Narragansett when the Pilgrims landed in New England in 1635. In 1636, Roger Williams acquired land use rights to Providence from the Narragansett Sachems.

The colonists quickly came into contact with both the Narragansett and Niantic Sachems, most notably Ninigret.

The Narragansett and Europeans maintained good relations until King Philips War in 1675-76.

In 40 years time, friendship between the Races deteriorated into hostility and war.

In 1675, the Narragansett allied themselves with King Philip and the Wampanoag Sachem, to support the Wampanoag Tribe's efforts to reclaim land in Massachusetts.

This war was the last major effort by the Indians of Southern New England to drive out the English settlers who wanted more Indian land. But the Narragansett were completely defeated. For, a military force of Puritans from Plymouth, Massachusetts Bay, and Connecticut declared war.

The United Colonies of New England raised a brigade of one thousand men and sent them to attack the Narragansett at the Great Swamp in West Kingston.

On a bitter cold December 19th, 1675 the troops marched and came upon a fortress containing six hundred lodges.

The soldiers poured into the Narragansett's fort. The vengeful colonists massacred about six hundred Braves, women, children and Elders. They were burned to death in their lodges.

The fighting became hand to hand. Gradually, the Narragansett gave ground and were defeated. A few escaped deep into the forest and swamp lands.

Many who refused to be subjected to the authority of the United Colonies left the area or were hunted down and killed. Some were sold into slavery in the Caribbean, others migrated to Upstate New York and many went to Brothertown, Wisconsin.

After the war, the remaining Narragansett were forced to live on reservation lands.

Due to the increase in number of Colonists, the Narragansett hunting and farming grounds were greatly depleted.

Colonists also introduced the common hog to the area. These domesticated hogs would roam along the coast and dig up the clam beds, a traditional food source for the Indians.

The tribe was under great pressure to abandon the traditional ways and adopt Waumpeshau (white man) ideas of civilization. As a result of dealing with the Waumpeshau, many debts were incurred which were paid off by land grants.

In 1790, the U.S. Congress introduced and passed the

Non-Intercourse Act, which prohibited the taking of Indian lands as payment for debts incurred.

During the 18th century, reservation life was extremely harsh. The State abolished the position of the Sachem, the traditional tribal leader, and took over the affairs of the tribe with a five-man council in 1792. However, tribal members continued to recognize the Sachems and traditional leadership.

By the end of the 18th century, the reservation, which is located near Charleston, Rhode Island had been reduced to 15,000 acres.

The Narragansett leaders resisted attempts by outsiders to take their remaining 15,000 acres of their reservation lands.

Then the State of Rhode Island illegally "detribalized" the Narragansett Tribe without federal sanction during the period of 1880-1884.

Even with the "detribalization" the Narragansetts continued to maintain their tribal customs and traditions and in the year 1901, there continued to be several leaders who were recognized both by the community and by outsiders as Narragansett tribal leaders.

In December of 1934 the Narragansett tribe of Indians was incorporated. The public once again recognized the offices of the Chief Sachem, Medicine Man, a nine-member Council, and Scribe and the office of the Prophet were re-established.

Then in the early 1940s the Narragansett Indians built their Longhouse which became the center of tribal activities.

In the year 1974, the tribe filed a land claim suit against the State of Rhode Island and several landowners for the return of approximately 3,200 acres of undeveloped Reservation lands

Their suit eventually concluded in an out-of-court settlement in 1978 of approximately 1,800 acres.

A fifteen-volume petition for Federal Recognition was submitted to the Department of the Interior, Bureau of Indian Affairs in 1979.

Then at long last, on April 11th, 1983 the Narragansett Indian Tribe received federal recognition and acknowledgement!

It took decades but their persistence at getting back a part of what belonged to them finally paid off. Here is where their heritage will live forever.

CHAPTER THREE

A Pequot Chief
"Narragansett Squaw Marries"

Au-camp-pa-chaug Sag Gunsh my fifteenth Great Grandmother was the daughter of the Narragansett Sachem, Weeroum. She left Rhode Island and moved to Mohegan.

Here she became a great Queen. For she married the Pequot Sachem Tamaquashad.

Sachem Tamaquashad had decreed to keep the royal blood within the realm of the Mohegan and Pequot. Tamaquashad's band left their ancient homes on the banks of the Hudson River.

Driven out by the Mohawks, Tamaquasha and his Band fought their way southward through Connecticut. They conquered the Native tribes as they came.

The Sachem made their headquarters near the present site of New London, though their main forts and villages were located in what is now known as the town of Groton near Mystic.

Sachem Tamaquashad was killed in battle and his son Muckquantdowas inherited the Sachem title role.

CHAPTER FOUR

"A Pequot Sachem" & His Family

My fourteenth Great Grandfather, Muckquantdowas lived in the Pequot village called "Awcumbucks"/ Aukumbumsk, which was situated in the heart of Pequot Country in Connecticut. (Near Gale Ferry).

The real territory of the Pequot was a narrow strip of coast in New London County, extending from the Niantic River to the Rhode Island boundary.

Comprising the present towns of New London, Groton, and Stonington. They also extended a few miles into Rhode Island to the Wecapaug River.

The Pequot; "Paquatauog", Indians, were an agricultural people who raised corn, beans, squash and tobacco.

They hunted and fished in the winter. Clothing and housing were similar, buckskin and semi-permanent villages of medium-sized longhouses and wigwams.

The Pequot, meaning; "Destroyer" were a Warlike Nation. They spoke the Algonquin dialect which was spoken by the Mohegan and the Narragansett People.

They, an Algonquian tribe of Connecticut were the most dreaded of the southern New England tribes. Unlike many other tribes, the Pequot were highly organized with a central authority which rested within the tribal council and ultimately the Grand Sachem.

Sachem Muckquantdowas later married a Royal Pequot Squaw by the name of Meekunump. Together they had three children all born in the village of Aukumbumsk, CT.

A son, Ahadon, a daughter named after her Mother, Meekunump (She the Mother of Uncas) and my thirteenth Great Grandfather, Woipequand.

Woipequand was born about 1496 in the Pequot village Aukumbumsk and he became Pequot Sachem after the death of his Father. Woipequand married his Narragansett Great Aunt Wekoum and they had two sons; Owaneco and Wopigwooit.

The future Fathers of Uncas and Sassacus.

CHAPTER FIVE

"Pequot Grand Sachem"

Pequot Sachem Wopigwooit, my twelfth Great Grandfather, was born in the year 1516 in Stonington CT. He married and had four sons and one daughter.

Wopigwooit dwelt in a large fort on what is now known as Pequot Hill in the town of Groton near Mystic.

Sachem Wopigwooit's eldest son, Tatobam otherwise called Sassacus was to become the future Pequot Grand Sachem.

At the time of their first contact with the Europeans, both Pequot and the Mohegan was originally a single tribe, which migrated to Eastern Connecticut from the upper Hudson Valley in New York sometime around 1500.

However in the 16th century there was an argument between Sassacus the Pequot leader and Uncas, the son of his Uncle Owanceo. (Uncas was also Sassacus' son-in-law.)

Uncas argued that he had greater ancestral descent and should have been given the throne after Wopigwooit's death. For Wopigwooit was murdered unwisely by Dutch Traders

Because in a desperate attempt by the Pequots to regain their trade monopoly lost to other tribes, they attacked and killed some Narragansetts attempting to trade at a Dutch trading outpost called; "The House of Hope."

But the resident trader for the Dutch West India Company, Jacob Elekens, had grown annoyed with the Pequots efforts to monopolize the fur trade and to retaliate, he seized the Pequot Sachem and threatened to kill him unless the Pequot ended their harassment and paid a ransom for his release.

The Pequot brought one hundred forty fathoms of wampum to the Post for the Sachem's release, which Elekens accepted but having expected beaver rather than these strange little shell beads he killed the Pequot Sachem.

This conflict, along with a smaller disagreement over trade, eventually caused Uncas to leave the Pequot Nation and he took the Pro-English trade of the Nation with him. (Leaving the Pro- Dutch trade behind)

Uncas had plans that clashed with the Grand Sachem Sassacus' strategy in dealing with the Europeans. He was concerned that the only way for his people to survive inevitable violence with the Europeans (and to prevent being swallowed up by them) was to try to create a peaceful alliance with them.

Uncas broke clan ties with the Pequot and led his followers west of the Thames River and settled at Shantok, the ancestral land of his Father's. They adopted the tribe's original name "Mohegan", meaning; "Wolf People".

The Pequot and Mohegan people were one tribe which now split into two. After the separation of the tribes, the Pequot still numbered about three thousand.

The next Sachem of the Pequot tribe could have been either Uncas or Sassacus because of their blood lines.

But most of the tribe wanted the leadership to go to Sassacus. So, the English faction under the leadership of Uncas left the main group and set up their own village.

During the winter of 1633-34 a major smallpox epidemic ravaged the tribes, especially affecting the Pro-Dutch band.

Within two years hostilities between these Pequot and the English had erupted into open warfare.

By the late 1630s, the English had emigrated from England to Massachusetts, ten thousand of them by 1634 expanded south and east to Connecticut, the territory of the powerful Pequots.

The Pequots did not welcome English intruders.

The New England Natives were untrusting of Europeans due to their hostile contact with outsiders since 1497.

Still remembering the expedition of Captain Thomas Hunt in 1614, who captured twenty-seven people (including Squanto) to sell into slavery, the aboriginal people had good reason to suspect the English of ominous deceit.

Anticipating trouble, the English had hired Lion Gardiner, a firey red head who stood six feet two inches tall, to build a fort, which was called Saybrook, at the mouth of the Connecticut River.

But hostilities became open warfare when the Pequots attacked the English settlement at Wethersfield and killed nine people.

CHAPTER SIX

"Tatobam / Sassacus"

My eleventh Great Grandfather, Tatobam otherwise known as Sassacus, which means: "He is Wild", led the Pequot Wars of 1636-37. He the eldest of five children had wed in the year 1555, at the age of nineteen.

Sassacus' bride was twenty-two year old Princess. She was the daughter of Sachem Ninigret and Herman Garrett's Sister.

Sachem Sassacus occupied a fort on what is now known as Fort Hill near the present Thames River, in the Pequot Village of Noank Point. The ancestral Pequot territory of Mistick, Quinnehtukqut (Mystic, Connecticut).

Sachem, Sassacus became a most noted Warrior. He was cool, calculating, treacherous, haughty, and fierce and malignant. He ruled over twenty-six subordinate chiefs and claimed control over all Connecticut east of the Connecticut River and the coast westward to the vicinity of Guilford or New Haven, while all of Long Island except the extreme west part was also under his dominion.

Sassacus reigned as Paramount leader during the Pequot War, such a devastating period of destruction and extermination of the Pequot by the colonists.

On May 26th, 1637, the English sent a Military force under Captains John Mason and John Underhill with a force of more than three hundred men to attack the Pequot Village. Their principal fort, near Mystic River, was surprised and set on fire.

The awaken Pequots shouted, Owanux! Owanux! (Englishmen! Englishmen!)

They mounted a valiant defense. But because of the fire their bowstrings caught fire, and they could no longer use bows and arrows. They had no distance weapons and therefore, they had to fight with ax and knife, hand-to- hand, a very unequal combat. As the battle was going on, Pequot men were running out with their clothes on fire attacking the English hand to hand.

But within an hour, the village burned and men, women and children perished in the flames or were shot down while trying to escape.

This terrible slaughter so crippled the Pequot that after a last few desperate but unsuccessful efforts at resistance, they decided to separate into smaller parties and abandon their country.

The Pequot scattered across what is now Southern New England, Long Island and Upstate New York.

Determined to end the Pequot, Captain John Mason and his troops pursued the remaining Pequots down the coast.

The Pequot Sachem Sassacus with four hundred souls, fled west to the Connecticut River where he killed three White Men, split their bodies open and hung them on trees as a message to the English.

Finally, the English caught up and a battle brought casualties to both sides.

The Pequots continued on to "Pequannock" (Stratford) to a village called "Uncoa" (Fairfield), a place of about twenty wigwams.

The English found the Pequots hiding in Sasco Swamp. The Warriors were slaughtered, except for Sassacus and eighty of his own warriors who managed to break free.

Sassacus and his followers fled west, hoping to gain refuge among the Mohawk. The Pequot had no sooner reached the Mohawk village, than, without being allowed to speak in council, he and most of his warriors were killed.

For the Mohawk had seen the display of English power and chose instead to kill Sassacus and his warriors, sending Sassacus' scalp to Hartford as a symbolic offering of Mohawk friendship with the English Colony on July 28th. 1637.

Sachem Sassacus' two surviving brothers were among the Pequots that were harbored by Sachem Ninigret, the Pequot Sachem's Father-in- Law.

Sassacus' brother, Sacowawen later on married Weuenquesh, she one of the daughters of Ninigret. They resided in Charlestown, Washington, Rhode Island.

The War officially ended September of 1638 when the few survivors of the Pequot Tribe were forced to sign the Treaty of Hartford declaring the Pequot Nation to be dissolved and the Pequot were dismembered.

Many of the tribal members were killed and others placed in slavery to Bermuda and the West Indies, or under the control of other tribes.

Those placed under the rule of the Mohegan's were separated into small groups.

These eventually became known as the Mashantucket (Western) Pequot, Ledyard. They were given back property in the year 1666 at Mashantucket and the Pawcatuck (Eastern) Pequot Lantern Hill 1683.

In the ensuing decades, the Pequot battled to keep their land.

By the beginning of the 17th century, European Monarchs had staked claim to the entire east coast.

European Colonists arrived believing they had the right to settle on land that was already inhabited by Native people.

For many Colonists who came to New England, a critical component of owning land was "improving" it; clearing and fencing it. And either planting crops or grazing animals.

Since the land appeared unoccupied to them... It did not resemble a farmscape – Colonists believed that no one owned it.

But in fact.... Native People did improve the landscape in ways that suited their own needs.

For example; Controlled burning of underbrush created a habitat that attracted deer for hunting and encouraged berry bushes to grow.

Sadly.........

To Europeans it seemed that Natives did not own the land they occupied.

PART TWO

"LONG ISLAND"

The Native Americans called it; "Paumonacke", land of tribute.

The Dutch called it; "Lange Eylandt." – 1614

British Settlers later called it; "Long Island".

"My Ancestor's Native Language"

From Southeastern Massachusetts, between the eastern shore of Narragansett Bay in Rhode Island to the western end of Cape Cod, the language spoken was an Algonquin north dialect.

The Wampanoag, Narragansett, Mohegan and Pequot people also spoke this dialect.

The Matinecock tribe from Flushing Bay to Smithtown Long Island spoke Algonquin with a Lenni- Lenape dialect.

The Montaukett, Unkechaugs and Shinnecock tribes spoke an Algonquin root.

Meat; Weeowa	Pot; Coquees
Stone; Sun	Bed; Apunna
Clay; Puckwe	Axe; Ochegan
Sand; Yaa	House; Weecho
Water; Nup	Door; Squnt
Dirt; Puckwe	Chimney; Hamanek
Sky; He-isk	Gourd; Whorammok

Cloud; Pama-Yauxen

Rain; Sukerun

Snow; Souchpo

Ice; Copatn

Hail; Mosecan

Sun; Haquaqua

Moon; Neepa

Star; Arequsac

Fire; Ruht

Whale; Puttap

Whale Oil; Puttapapum

Geese; Pum

Milk; Wampachuunk

Beans; Mais-Cusseet

Black; Shickayo

White; Wampayo

Red; Squayo

Watermelon; Waghti-Whorammok

Wampum; Whampump

Moccasin; Mocussenus

Good; Woreecan

Bad; Mattateayah

Clever; Weayuh

Handsome; Woresco

Ugly; Neehowuchayuh

Cross Fellow; Cheeascoto

River; Seepus

Ocean; Cutstuk

Bay; Petapach

Walk Down; Cutcheepun

To Sit; Klummatap

To Run; Quaquees

To Break; Pwksa

To Bend; Co-Unkarunneman

Yellow; Weesa- Wayo

Blue; Seewamp-wayo

Green; Uscusquayo

Rainbow; Papuhmuhcsunc

Bow; Atump

Arrow; Neep

Tomahawk; Chekenas

I; Nee

Thou; Kee

He; Naacum

Small; Peewatsu

One; Naquut

Two; Nees

Three; Nus

Four; Yaut

Five; Napaa

Six; Nacuttah

Seven; Tumpawa

To Cut With A Knife; Poquesimman

To Cut with an Axe; Poquesahaman

To Kill; Wuhnsa

War; Ayutowac

Peace; Weehsaac

To Hunt; Peensaac

Blanket; Aqueewants

Sunchem; King

Saeunskq; Queen

Wewanchum; Corn

Mausqueseets; Beans

Ausqoote; Pumpkins

Quauhaug; Hard Clam

Suxawaug; Long Clam

Niep; Water

Eage; Land

Mashnee; Canoe

Mashmanock

Eight; Swats

Nine; Nwre

Ten; Payac

God; Manto

A Great God; Masakeetmund

Devil; Mattateashet

Thunder; Pataguahamoc

Lighting; Wowosumpa

Merosuck; Canoe Place

Niamuck; Between Fishing Places

Paumanock; Land of Tribute

"Brothers, we must be one as the English are, or we shall soon all be destroyed. You know our Fathers had plenty of deer and skins; our plains were full of deer and turkeys, and our coves and rivers were full of fish.

But, brothers, since these English have seized upon Our country, they cut down the grass with scythes, and the trees with axes.

Their cows and horses eat up the grass, and their hogs spoil our beds of clams; and finally we shall starve to death. Therefore, I beseech you to act like men. All the Sachems both to the east and west have joined with us And we are resolved to fall upon them."

Narragansett Chief, Sachem Miantonmo's speech to the Long Island Indians 1638

CHAPTER SEVEN

"Pequot Squaw" & Montauk Chief

Quashawam, my tenth Great Grandmother was born in the year 1556 in Groton Connecticut. She, the daughter of Pequot Sachem, Sassacus.

Quashawam ran away to Montauk Long Island at the age of fourteen. There she married nineteen year old Mongotucksee. He, one of the sons of Sachem Sowheag, Chieftain of a distinct tribe, under the name "Wangunks".

Mongotucksee, Chief Long Knife to his tribe the Montauketts, was proud and despotic in peace and terrible in war. Although a tyrant of his people, he protected them from their enemies and commanded their respect for his savage virtues.

The Montauketts, the most powerful tribe of all Long Island, lived in the area now known as East Hampton, their territory extended to Montauk Point.

Their language was of an Algonquin root, which was also spoken by the other eastern Long Island tribes.

They were tall, of proud and lofty movement, of active bodies and as straight as the arrow.

Their chiefs and their braves were distinguished above those of the other tribes of the island for prowess in the field; for a recklessness of life in battle, and for the bold and daring onset with which, under their war scream, they would rush upon an enemy.

The Narragansett and the Mohawks yielded to Mongotucksee's prowess. The ancestors of the last of the Mohegan have trembled at the expression of his anger. He sustained his power not less by the resources of his mind than the vigor of his arm.

Chief Long Knife was seven feet tall and considered a giant. He with his men, the Montauketts, built what was the forerunner of the Shinnecock Canal, for the purpose of passing their canoes from one bay to the other.

Mongotucksee's Mother, born in Mattabeseck, (Middletown) Connecticut, was the daughter and heiress of a deceased Sachem. For it was through her, that he obtained his land, Montauk; meaning: "Uncertain".

Before the arrival of the Europeans the Montauketts located their villages along the banks of freshwater streams and tidal bays in the costal areas on the southern fork of eastern Long Island.

This rich ecosystem provided them with both woodland plants and animals and a wide variety of shellfish and sea mammals.

The Montauketts made disk-shaped beads from quahog shells, which they used for trade and for tribute payments to the Niantics of Southern New England.

Purple beads made from the outer lip of the quahog were in great demand, particularly among the inland tribes. They began to make cylindrical beads and weaved them into wampum, which was used as currency.

The Montaukett's rise to prominence was based on the importance of wampum, the chief means of barter between Indian tribes.

Although the largest tribe on Long Island the Montauketts were no match for the larger, more aggressive tribes of Connecticut and Rhode Island.

The Niantics of Southern New England in particular, preyed on the Montauketts, slipping across the Long Island Sound in their silent war canoes, to raid at will. The Montauketts were forced to pay tribute to the Niantics in wampum.

CHAPTER EIGHT

"Chief Long Knife Mongotucksee" & Quashawam

Mongotucksee and Quashawam were the Parents of the four Long Island Sachems, Poggatticut, Wyandanch, Momoweta and Nowedonah, my ninth Great Grandfather.

They also had a daughter, named after her Mother, Quashawam.

Wyandanch, meaning; "Wise Speaker" became Chief of the Montaukett's under his Father guidance.

At that time, Wyandanch was a young and ambitious Sachem, he a tall man with black hair and black eyes.

Wyandanch had become through the years, spokesperson for his family in their efforts to free themselves from the Niantics and their Sachem Ninigret's tyranny.

The young Sachem and his brothers and sister lived in a palisaded village on the high bluffs of present day Montauk Point.

Wyandanch married at the age of twenty-eight, to his Queen, Wicchitaubit. She was a royal race of the Iroquois. They settled in a dense forest known as Heather Woods.

Together, they had a son, Wyancombone, and a daughter, Quashawam, whom the English called Heather Flower.

CHAPTER NINE

"The year 1637"

Wyandanch the now sixty-five year old Sachem learned of the Pequot Massacre and went to Fort Saybrook on May 29th, 1637 and requested a meeting with Lion Gardiner, the Chief Commander.

Wyandanch wanted to create his own direct alliance with Gardiner. He wanted to assure the English that, in spite of his kinship and Historic ties with the Pequot, the Montauketts wanted friendly relations with the victors.

The Montaukett Sachem was the family's representative for a carefully thought out plan to prementaly free Paumanack from their ancient enemy, the Narragansett of Rhode Island and to establish direct family control over European trade goods on eastern Long Island.

For the Niantics grew insatiable in their demands for wampum, and Wyandanch quickly realized he must put an end to this drain on his tribe.

So, Wyandanch negotiated an alliance with Gardiner. The Sachem decided that it was in the best interest of his people to side with the English.

Wyandanch's fears of the Narragansett were well founded. For, Ninigret, a fierce an ambitious Niantic Sachem, leader of a Southern branch of the Narragansett, intended to replace the Pequot influence on Long Island with his own.

Gardiner told the Montaukett Sachem, that he had to show good faith by helping the English troops hunt down all the Pequot's on Long Island, who killed Englishmen.

(According to rumor, Sachem Sassacus and a large number of Pequot's had fled to Long Island).

Gardiner's charge to Wyandanch put him in a difficult position because the Montaukett are close relatives of the Pequot and Pequot could be found in nearly every village on eastern Long Island.

Wyandanch's brother, Sachem Poggaticut, protected the Pequot. Poggaticut did not oppose an alliance with the English but he was unwilling to cooperate in the killing of the Pequot.

Mean while Wyandanch continued to be pressed by the Narragansett. In 1653 Ninigret attacked, killing thirty people in what came to be known as Massacre Valley. The name given to the low-lying land just east of Fort Hill.

Ninigret took fourteen prisoners including two Sachems and Wyandanch's daughter Quashawam.

Sachem Ninigret, who resided east of the Pawcatuck River, had hoped to break the new formed alliance between the Montauketts and the English.

The old enemy shunned alliances with the English and claimed that the raid was to avenge the murder of one of his men by Wyandanch, several years earlier. In October of 1654, Gardiner obtained the release of the Montaukett Sachem's daughter.

For Quashawam was held for ransom. Gardiner sent sums of wampum to Ninigret in an effort to gain Wyandanch's daughter's return. This gesture forged a strong friendship with Wyandanch.

Wyandanch, in the same year became the Leader of all the tribes on Long Island following the death of his eldest brother, Poggatticut.

It was in Lion Gardiner's interest to assist the Montaukett Sachem to retrieve his daughter, thus placing Wyandanch in the position of obligation and debt.

Gardiner also knew that his support would strengthen Wyandanch's influence among the Sachems on Long Island.

When Ninigret threatened again in 1655, Gardiner was able to obtain English Naval protection for Wyandanch.

With the English support, Wyandanch further strengthened his influence all the way to the Shinnecock territory and through western Long Island.

The East Hampton authorities proclaimed Wyandanch "Grand Sachem" of Long Island. A title which served their interest because they could bypass the local Sachems and buy large tracts of land from Wyandanch.

By 1658 the English were requiring Wyandanch's signature on all deeds. This was confirmed when Wyandanch rewarded Lion Gardiner with a thirty-thousand tract of land in the area of Smithtown.

CHAPTER TEN

"Montaukett Sunk Squaw" Wicchitaubit

Wyandanch died sometime during the fall of 1659 at the age of eighty-six. Though not recorded it is possible he died in the Plagues, which took the lives of many.

An estimated two-thirds of the Algonquin people on Long Island, between 1659 and 1664 had died.

Wyandanch was buried at Montauk, next to his brother, Poggatticut.

Scarcely was the Sachem laid to rest, than the hand of greed nerved by the tempter of mankind was outstretched to bring about the sale of Montauk.

The death of Wyandanch encouraged both the English and the Niantic's to take advantage of the Montaukett's during the transition to new leadership.

Wyandanch's widow emerged as Sunksquaw of the Montauketts during these troubled times.

Wyandanch's son was too young to assume a leadership role. The Sunksquaw was a principal party in five major transactions. These documents have always named her son, Wyancombone as well.

With the death of Wyandanch and a devastating epidemic it left the Montauketts weak and demoralized.

Ninigret, their old nemesis, took advantage of the situation by launching a series of attacks which forced the Montauketts to seek refuge in East Hampton.

The Montaukett Sunksquaw, her son and three advisors turned to East Hampton for help, as Wyandanch had done after Ninigret's raid in 1653.

This time however, the English refused to protect the village on Montauk from attack. The English told the Montauketts that they must leave their homes and take temporary refuge within the bounds of East Hampton.

In February 1662 Gardiner and his colleagues pressed the Montauketts for a gift to show their gratitude for the sanctuary provided by the Town.

Gardiner asked them to give a small tract of land called (Hither) Heather Woods. The forty-two hundred acre extends from Napeague eastward to Fort Pond.

According to Benjamin and Stephen Pharaoh, two Montaukett's testimonies, the East Hampton Officials took advantage of the desperate plight of the Montauketts.

The East Hampton men wrote the deed with a purpose beyond the straightforward description of the transaction itself.

Persuasion had been brought upon Wicchitaubit and her young son, which they could not bear.

They did not take kindly to the sale of their ancestral home.

The Montauketts were disinherited of their domain. Heart stricken and life weary in the realization of what her relinquishment had cost her people; Wicchitaubit was laid to rest beside her husband.

CHAPTER ELEVEN
"Wyancombone"

After the death of his Father Wyandanch in 1659, Wyancombone came to reside on the Calf Pasture, south of Main Street, as a refuge from the persecution of the Narragansett. The Montauketts settled on Indian Field, north of what is now Deep Hollow Ranch.

While there in 1662, Small Pox raged to threaten their extinction and Wyancombone then died at the age of twenty-two.

CHAPTER TWELVE
"Princess Heather Flower" Quashawam

Three days after the burial of the young Sachem, Quashawam inherited her Father's position.

This left Quashawam as the only surviving member of Wyandanch's immediate family.

But the loss of her Parents and brother within a relatively short time was unsettling to her

Thus began challenges for the Grand Sachem title and asserting rights to his land.

Quashawam's husband was Poniute, a fierce Montaukett Anti-English Sagamore. They had a son, Poniute, who called himself "Mousup" and later adopted the name Wyandanch after his Grandfather. They lived in a village on the west bank of Three Mile Harbor.

The English recognized Quashawam as the Montaukett Sunksquaw in 1663. But she exorcised a dormant role in community decisions. She was docile and peaceable.

But, Quashawam and the Montauketts did successfully challenge the boundaries of the purchase of land from Lion Gardiner to Richard Smith.

Between Quashawam and the Town of East Hampton, Governor Nicolls settled a long standing dispute over the boundaries.

The Governor affirmed Quashawam's rights to the Montauk homeland on the eastern end of Long Island an area about four thousand acres.

But by the end of 1663 the Montauketts had lost a large portion of their land.

In 1665, Richard Nicolls, who was the first Governor of the newly established colony of New York, officially declared that there was no longer any "Grand Sachem" of Long Island.

Every Sachem, said the Governor, shall keep his particular property over his people as formerly. The English, who had created the position, had now abolished it.

Quashawam disappeared from the colonial records soon after her settlement with the Governor for she died about 1669.

By 1700 the English had taken possession of the Montaukett's lands, leaving the Indians with only residence rights to a small area near the present day village of Montauk.

And by the 1790s very little of their Algonquin Language had survived.

Every aspect of the Montaukett's lives had changed. Their language, their customs, how they viewed the world, how they worshiped their God, all of it gone.

Their Reservation on Montauk Point shrank as more of their land was brought up by their East Hampton neighbors in questionable land deals.

There began a rapid decline and only about one hundred sixty-two Montauketts remained.

Several Montaukett families followed Samson Occom, the Mohegan Missionary, to join his Christian Indian Community at Brothertown in Central New York State.

In 1849 Arthur Benson, a wealthy developer from Brooklyn, conspired to evict the Montauketts from their homeland, the Indian Fields.

Some Montauketts had moved to places on Long Island and southern New England where they could find work.

But the remaining Montauketts continued trapping fur animals for their pelts, shooting fowl, harvesting oysters, raising their stock and gardens. Their ice was harvested at the ponds in winter; berries were picked and sold for money for shoes. They continued their craft work, making bowls, squaw brooms, scrubs and baskets, all on their ancestral land at Indian Fields. Their Reservation life continued on.

Some of the Montaukett men worked for the East Hamptoners. They were Fence Keepers of the livestock pastured at Montauk and laborers for the Gardiners' and others.

They used traditional woodworking skills to make pig pens, ladles and bowls for Settlers homes. They provided fish, oysters and game for them. As skilled Shore Whalers, Montaukett men were fought over by Entrepreneurial East Hamptoners to be their crewmen.

The Native women worked, using the spinning wheel to spin yarn, a necessity for all knitwear and weaving of essential cloth.

They became expert makers of butter and cheese, which were major cash crops for their masters.

Baskets, scrubs, jellies and fine hand work provided cash for themselves. They cared for the Mother's children of colonial families.

The Benson family, who had bought the whole Montauk Peninsula from the Town Trustees, used it as a hunting preserve and planned to develop it.

But the Montauketts stood in their way. For their village was smack in the middle of Frank Benson's plans!

Promises he made to the Montauketts were empty ones. For he told the Indians if they would give up their land, they could return in the summer, would get a yearly annuity, and education for their children.

But, their homes at Indian Field containing their Deeds and Records were burned, and they were driven away from their ancestral home.

CHAPTER THIRTEEN

"Brothers: David" And Stephen Talkhouse Pharaoh

In 1869, David Pharaoh, Chief of the Long Island Tribe preserved a form of tribal organization into the 19th century and retained their hereditary chiefs until his death about 1875.

After David's death, Maria, his wife and their children could not maintain the homesteading lifestyle. They were lured to move to Freetown, north of East Hampton Village.

They too, lost their home, their ancestral land from false promises made to them.

David's brother, Stephen Talkhouse Pharaoh had joined together with him to fight the force of sale of their land, Indian Fields.

For Stephen, it was a place of memory and history. It was all he had ever known.

David passed away leaving Stephen to fight alone. A year later what little remained of the Montaukett's world was about to be replaced by a new and emerging Long Island.

Even as the tiny Montaukett community was fighting to stay at Indian Fields, eighty miles to the west, in the Hempstead Plains, a New York City Businessman had already built a planned community called Garden City.

Long Island would never be the same. After Stephen Talkhouse Pharaoh died in the year 1879, the Government policy was based on the premise that the Native Americans would be better off if they abandoned their traditional Indian identity and assimilated into the mainstream population.

The once powerful Montauketts lost legal status as a tribe in 1909.

The Montauketts were devastated. They tried to regain their land up until 1917 which bankrupted them.

The Indians were pressured to divide up their Reservation into individual homesteads and live like their white neighbors.

CHAPTER FOURTEEN

"Chief Wyandank Pharaoh"

On November 17th 1910, seventy-five Montauketts along with their Chief, Wyandank Pharaoh, were told by the State Supreme Court Justice Abel Blackmar, that the Tribe did not exist.

The Montaukett tribe of Indians had been disintegrated and had been absorbed into the mass of citizens.

He stated; "There was no tribe of Montauk Indians". Blackmar said, they had no internal government and they lived a sort of shiftless life, hunting, fishing, and cultivating the ground and often leaving Montauk for long periods and working in some menial capacity.

He concluded, that the Montauketts no longer lived as a tribe and no longer enjoyed any political or civil rights as a tribe.

For Blackmar, found agreement with the Benson's. All the Montauketts rights, titles, interests, and claims to the rights and privileges in the land known as Montauk Point was released.

This is how the Montauketts lost their land.

The Montauketts had to adapt to the forces of change. However they clung tenaciously to their identity.

Today, the Montaukett Tribe has withdrawn from the public eye to focus on strategies designed to strengthen their tribal structure.

CHAPTER FIFTEEN
"Shelter Island" Grand Sachem Poggaticutt

Mongotucksee's eldest son, Poggaticutt ruled the Manhansett Indians of Shelter Island or as the Indians called it; "Manhansack-aha-quash-awamock", meaning; An Island Sheltered by Islands, after his Father's rein as Sachem.

The Manhansetts also called; "The People of the Dancing Meadow" lived on Ram Island and Hog Island. Eighty thousand acres of land marsh and mist nestled between the North and South Forks of Long Island. They too spoke the Algonquin root dialect like their relations, the Montauketts. Their Grand Sachem Poggaticutt lived on Carp Meadow.

Poggaticutt was a great Sachem. He was very distinguished, a man of his people. Well loved, respected and obeyed.

He was an Aristocrat, and belonged to the royal family of Indians. He was not only the Chief of the Manhansett tribe but was the Grand Sachem of all the tribes of Long Island.

The Manhansett were a peaceful tribe that embraced both the Montauketts and the Mohawks.

They had a peaceful and bountiful life, since the Island was protected from the worst of weather by the sheltering arms of Long Island's North and South Forks. The surrounding waters yielded up a bounty of fish and water fowl, while the woods and fields were equally stocked with deer and other game.

Poggaticutt, meaning; "Wise Man" was a great Statesman, a wise Councilor, and a profound Philosopher and Nobleman.

Sachem Poggaticutt and his Queen, Ligomee, Had a son, Yo-kee who succeeded his Father as Sachem.

Now, while the early settlers arrived from England seeking a haven for practicing their Religion, the first Europeans to settle on Shelter Island were wealthy Sugar Merchants from Barbados.

They came seeking the stands of white oak to use for their barrels.

In 1652, the year that Shelter Island was settled by the English, a dispute arose as to the rights of the Island.

The Manhansett claimed that in a conveyance made some years previous, they did not relinquish all their rights in the Island, but only a certain portion which was marked by some trees.

The tribe tried to fight for their ancestral home land. They sent the Sachem's brother-in-law, Cockenoe DelongIsland to Hartford as their Representative, to plead their case before the Commissioners of the United Colonies of New England.

Alas, this beautiful gem of the sea was once home to the Manhansett Tribe of Indians.

The Island became thickly populated and the Indians were thinly scattered all over.

To the very last hour of his life, the eighty-three year old Sachem Poggaticutt had steadily opposed the sale of the land of his tribe. In the year 1653, the Grand Sachem of "Paum-man-ake" passed away.

All that night the tribes mourned their fallen leader, but at first light the procession resumed towards the far Hills of Montauk.

For his remains were transported for burial from Shelter Island to Montauk.

The entire tribe traveled by large canoes from Shelter Island to North Haven, They then walked the rest of the way to the burial ground of their beloved Sachem.

How sad, the land of his Fathers', Warriors of a most peaceful tribe, that he, Poggaticutt an aged King, held onto with a firm grasp was signed away into sinewy hands.

Hence, this Isle of Shelter was settled and its original inhabitants were forced to relocate to the neighboring lands of Montauk and Shinnecock Tribes.

CHAPTER SIXTEEN

"Sachem (Paucamp) Momoweta"

Paucamp, the youngest brother of the Long Island Sachems, was born in the year 1574.

As a teenager, Paucamp traveled extensively with his Father, Mongotucksee, who ruled during the 1500s.

They would visit the neighboring islands and the continent, as far as Boston, and as far south as New York.

Their canoes traveled New Haven and the Connecticut River frequently, for Paucamp liked to circulate among his extended family, which was quite extensive.

Father and son's habits were social and they visited often. Also visiting neighboring tribes, with whom they delighted to mix in conversation and friendly gaiety.

Their canoes were of the largest class, and in some instances capable of carrying eighty persons.

It is said, Paucamp's brother, Wyandanch required the strength of seven or eight men to draw his canoe from the water upon the shore; and on one occasion was damaged at Gardiner's Island for want of a sufficient number of persons to place it beyond the reach of the sea.

CHAPTER SEVENTEEN
"Corchaug"

Long before the white man came to this area, the Corchaug (which Cutchogue gets its name) occupied the eastern end of Long Island, known as the North Neck.

The Corchaug, meaning; "Ancient Ones" were allied with the Shinnecock and Montauketts. They too spoke the Algonquin root dialect.

Paucamp also known as Momoweta, which means; "He Who Gathers" became Sachem after his Father's rule. Momoweta ruled Green Port, North Fork, Riverhead and Southold.

Paucamp married Mishcawa and had two children. A son Ambusco, who succeeded him as Sachem, and a daughter named Yoopsag.

Paucamp lived with his family at the foot of Pipe's Neck Road. Their dwelling was oval in shape made of saplings lashed together and covered with marsh hay. There was a fireplace in the center of the wigwam and a hole in the top which was plastered with clay to let the smoke out without danger of fire.

When the English arrived in the 1630s, they did everything they could to remove the Corchaug Indians.

Sachem Paucamp then in his early sixties went to meet with William Salmon and Matthew Sinderland, in Southold in 1638- 1640. He also had a meeting with Isaac de Rasiere of New Netherlands. But sadly, the Indians of this region exchanged the use of their land for protection from their enemies with the Europeans who had guns, metal weapons and other things of value.

The Colonists either misunderstood or ignored the Indian's concepts of land use and claimed ownership of the Indian lands and denied them access to them.

The Indians who formally occupied these lands were pushed out. Many enslaved.

Sachem Momoweta had passed away in the year 1665, at the age of ninety-one.

And as the Europeans population increased, Native People were pushed further off traditional lands. They were forced into farming, instead of their hunting, gathering ways of life.

Momoweta's daughter, Yoopsag moved to the South Harbor village. She refused to move to the Indian Neck site in 1690, when the remnant of the North Fork Indians were forced off land granted to them at a public meeting of Southolders.

In time, the Indians were displaced or destroyed. The last of their village disappeared around 1715.

CHAPTER EIGHTEEN
"The Long Island Indian Forts"

Each Long Island Tribe had a fort and the brothers, Poggaticutt, Wyandanch, Momoweta and Nowedonah communicated with each other by smoke signals.

The Montaukett's fort was one of the largest forts. It was built on the hill where the Montauk Manor now stands.

Fort Corchaug was built by the tribe. A rectangular palisade fort made of tall trees. The four walls of the fort were built as a refuge for the Indians.

With the salt creek on one side and farm fields of corn and beans on the other, this fed the Indians. The tribes built forts for protection from other Indian invasions and the English Military.

Fort Corchaug is the only fort that remains today and virtually untouched.

CHAPTER NINETEEN

"Shinnecock Sachem Nowedonah"

Nowedonah, my ninth Great, Grandfather, was the third brother of the four Long Island Sachems. He married Sabra "Sybel" Lott, a Montaukett Squaw in 1595. Both were twenty-three years old at the time.

They had but one child. A daughter named Jerusha, she who became a Squaw of great renown.

Nowedonah was born in Eaton's Neck in 1573. At the age of eighteen he was an avid Hunter and Fisherman. He used a bow and arrow, which was as tall as a man, to shoot deer and bear. He used various nets and traps for fishing. One of his methods was, to set up a net at the mouth of the creek or mud flat at high tide; when the tide started to go out, the fish coming out of the creek were caught in the net.

While hunting one day with a companion, he was kidnapped by the Shinnecock. The companion, who had escaped into the brushes, took word to Nowedonah's Father, Chief Long Knife Mongotucksee.

The fire signals went out and three hundred Montaukett Warriors were on their way to the Shinnecock village. The Montauketts stormed the fort and immediately made a decision that would determine future Long Island Indian Policy.

Wyandanch appointed Nowedonah to become the Sachem of Shinnecock. That's how the Shinnecock Tribe became apart of the Montaukett Confederacy. The Shinnecock were one of the thirteen original tribes of Long Island, which was called by the Indians, "Sewanaka", meaning: Land of Shells.

The men wore breech clothes at all times and added robes of fur and moccasins in the colder weather. They burned their hair off with hot rocks, leaving only a central comb of hair. Various feathers were also worn on the head. Children generally ran naked until puberty.

Shinnecock originally called: "Shinni-auk-it", Meaning: "At Sea Level" extended eastward to the Easthampton town line and westward to the Brookhaven town line, with the Atlantic Ocean to the south and the Peconic Bay to the north. The Shinnecock were also an Algonquin speaking people.

CHAPTER TWENTY

"Shinnecock and Settlers meet"

On June 12th, 1640, the sixty-seven year old Sachem Nowedonah, meaning: "The Seeker", saw a sloop approach the shore.

The small boat was carrying eight men, one woman and one child. The leader was Edward Howell, with him was his wife, Eleanor and their son Arthur. These occupants were English Puritans from Lynn Massachusetts.

They landed at Conscience Point. It was called this because upon landing, so tradition has it, the first woman to step ashore said, "For conscience sakes, we are on dry land at last"!

The Settlers found, (what was to become the town of Southampton) was owned by the Shinnecock Tribe, a peaceful, hardy group of four to five hundred Indians.

The group from Lynn Massachusetts had organized an expedition to settle at Long Island. The group devised a document called; "The Disposal of the Vessel" in that year of 1640.

The terms of the document stated that they would turn over to Daniel Howe their shares in the vessel that brought then to Lynn from England.

In exchange Howe was to transport them to Long Island where they would establish a settlement. Howe was also to make several more trips over the ensuring two years to bring additional settlers, for the settlers were attracted by the fertile soil and sandy beaches.

This unknown to the Shinnecock Sachem and his tribe, the men from the little vessel and the Great Sachem Nowedonah attempted a greeting.

The White man was not a strange thing to the Great Sachem, as his brother Wyandanch, Sachem of the Montuaketts and Lion Gardiner had become friends.

Likewise, Poggaticutt, his eldest brother, Sachem of the Manhansetts had met at council with another brother, Momoweta of the Corchaug, in the attempts to arrange for protection with the English, as early as 1624.

In a gesture of friendliness, the Shinnecock parceled out eight square miles of land to the Settlers, for sixteen coats and sixty bushels of corn, the latter to be paid after the harvest.

Their first lodgings were huts or holes in the ground about seven feet deep. With bark ceilings and bark and timber walls with log plank floors.

The Shinnecock shared with the Settlers, their knowledge of planting corn and fertilizing it with fish. Growing crops, digging clams & scallops from nearby Bays and trapping game.

The Indians showed them how to make heaps like molehills, each about two and a half feet from the others, which they planted Maize. In each heap went five or six grains.

Before the hard corn could be eaten, it had to be processed. The Indians had a "samp pounder", which was an oversized mortar and pestle that did the work.

The mortar was fashioned from a three-foot tree stump that was seared and scraped until a twelve to fifteen inch cavity was hollowed out. The spring pole to maneuver the pestle came from a nearby sapling, bent and poised over the mortar. The pestle itself was a long, heavy stick, rounded at the end and fastened to the spring pole.

To soften the corn, kernels were soaked overnight in water and lye, or hot ashes, then rinsed, dried and brought to the pounder.

Among the settlers, Autumn Saturdays on Long Island were samp days, when villages would cart their kernels to a central mortar. The thumping lasted into the early candlelight.

Though the settlers took many recipes from the Indians, none was more important than the recipe for samp porridge, a heavy, stick to your ribs corn, bean and meat stew. On its own, it was an everyday breakfast, lunch or dinner.

Most often though, samp was a moveable feast: Started on Saturday, it would simmer on the hearth all week, altered day by day with a bit of meat here, a drop of shellfish there. No one got bored. By the end of the week a popcorn flavored crust had formed around the pot. Each family member would try to lift out the whole shell without breaking it, and whoever did would receive special privileges.

CHAPTER TWENTY-ONE
"Whaling"

The Shinnecocks were among a handful of Native American tribes that actively hunted whales along the coast since 1620. They pursued the whales in as many as twenty dugout canoes carrying up to one hundred men that would hunt a single whale.

For whaling, they used harpoons and spears fashioned out of sharpened deer antlers and the bones of other whales.

When the English settlers first arrived here, they observed the native method of going after the whales that migrated close to shore.

Using the canoes, the Indians would stab the whales with spears and wait for them to die from loss of blood and then tow them to shore to be butchered. Or, they would harvest meat from beached whales, which was common.

The Indians would boil the blubber and mix the oil with their corn and beans. Or they would rub the oil into animal hides as a preservative. They kept the whale's tails and fins for ceremonial feasts. For these parts represented the power of the beasts.

It was not long before the Settlers formed their own whaling companies. . . .

The concept of land ownership was alien to the Indians. Initially the Indians exchanged the use of their lands for protection from their enemies by the Europeans.

But after the arrival of the English to Southampton, so began predetermined steps to secure title to Indian lands and to control the Indian population.

This way the settlers could start to develop communities of farmers and seafarers.

As the transformation from Indian land to an English community took place, conflicts arose between the two groups.

The English settlers allowed their hogs to range freely in the woods until harvest time when they brought them in to fatten them for slaughter. Occasionally, when the Indians came upon the hogs, they hunted them like wild game and killed them. This was most likely to happen whenever the Indians caught them rooting up their shellfish beds.

Cattle and horses also created problems. The Indians kept their winter food in storage pits near their wigwams.

When they moved to another location, they left the pits open. The English called these pits "Indian Barns" and their grazing livestock sometimes fell into the Indian's pits and injured themselves.

Another problem arose and caused friction between the two. With the increase of the English livestock, their cattle, horses and hogs were getting into the Indian corn fields and destroyed the crops. Fences, of course were an alien concept to the Indians.

But, the Shinnecock continued to plant their crops on land which was within the boundaries of the 1640 purchase.

The English did not protest until April of the next year, when their first town meeting assembled. They then began a systematic effort to buy Long Island land from the Sachems to preserve them for English settlements.

The Shinnecock soon found themselves tenants on their home soil!

The Indians assumed that they were merely granting the visitors a place to sit down and use the land for a while.

This understanding was consistent with aboriginal concepts of "property".

Land was "used" by the community; it was not something that one owned either individually or collectively.

The English principle of land ownership had no equivalent in Indian culture.

Their confinement led to regular boundary disputes between the Shinnecocks and their new neighbors.

Some English houses were set on fire by the Shinnecock as a protest against land seizures and laws that applied to only them; this led to penalties being assessed against the Shinnecocks. The Indians had no money to pay fines, but they had land, so the English seized more of it. Laws passed by the colonists had the effect of hemming the Shinnecock in and cutting them off from their traditional way of life.

They were forbidden from hunting or trapping on their former land; they were forbidden from gathering nuts in traditional areas; they were fined if the colonist's cattle fell through the Indian-built underground cellars; they were fined if they did not fence their fields and their dogs were shot.

By the year 1648 Southampton colony had moved from Olde Town Pond to Towne Street (present day, Main Street) and constructed their new homes.

The town's name was coined to honor the Earl of Southampton, Henry Wriothesly, who showed favor on the new American settlements. The settlers also built a meeting house which was used to conduct public business.

In the year 1656, the proprietors announced that no more wigwams could be built within the settlement's boundaries.

From this time on, the Indian way of life changed forever.

CHAPTER TWENTY-TWO

"Quashawam Sunksquaw"

Upon the death of the Great Sachem Nowedonah, at the age of ninety-four, his sister Quashawam became his successor in 1667.

Mongotucksee's only daughter, who was born in Eaton's Neck in 1575 took over as Chieftain of the Shinnecock Nation.

Quashawam, the Sunksquaw of the Shinnecock and sister of the four great Sachems, married Cockenoe De Long Island at the age of twenty-five in the year 1595.

Cockenoe was an Interpreter and Chief Counselor for the Montauketts. Together, he and Quashawam made their home at Shinnecock.

While living with his Sachem Squaw at Shinnecock, Cockenoe was taken into the house of the Sachems, and was entitled to be designated as a Sagamore.

But, Quashawam did not take an active role as Sachem, or in any negotiations. For Quashawam was ninety-two years old, and was Sunksquaw only because of her family bloodline.

The Mandush family asserted the Chief Sachem position, and the Montauketts over the Shinnecock was abandoned.

The Montauk Grand Sachem title was no longer evoked. It had lost all credibility.

Following the death of Quashawam, Cockenoe spent his last days at Montauk among the hills he loved so well.

Cockenoe and his Squaw Quashawam did not leave a direct heir to succeed them as leaders, of their tribe.

In 1671 the leadership of the Shinnecock was Pungamo, son of Chief Mandush.

In the year 1686 the authority to sell lands rested with the family and heirs of Mandush.

The English Colonists had viewed Indian culture as inferior and attempted to destroy it as quickly as they could.

At the start of the first white settlement, the Shinnecocks lost ground steadily.

During the seventeenth century the "uncivilized" aspects of Indian culture were used as a justification for taking away Indian land.

The colonists argued that because the Indians had no intention of making the land productive through application of agriculture and technology, they had forfeited their title.

By the early 1700s, the Shinnecocks were given rights to the wide, hilly neck east of the Shinnecock Canal, which was a place where they harbored their canoes

In 1703 tribal land was reduced to about 3,600 acres. Throughout this period, the Shinnecocks gradually entered the settlers' economy. Many worked as domestics on local estates, working side by side with African-American and white indentured servants.

Numerous unfair land transactions had by the 1800s reduced the tribe's holdings.

The English allowed their cattle and sheep to graze unattended in the hills, and they often destroyed the Indian's crops. In a case in 1853 two desperate Shinnecock men, Luther and James Bunn, impounded a herd of Goats owned by a wealthy white man named Austin Rose.

The two Indians were sued and forced to pay damages when the court ruled that they had been negligent in maintaining their fences.

In 1859, a group of private investors asked New York State to dismantle the 1703 deal and confine the tribe to its current 800-acre reservation on Shinnecock Bay.

So now the East End Farmers could begin to build their windmills to grind grain or pump water and their cattle could graze among the sand dunes, and their now fertile farms can grow quantities of potatoes.

At the end of the nineteenth century, the area became well-known for its summer vacationers and golfing began on a course in the Shinnecock Hills.

Southampton became a fashionable resort. It could be argued that no people ever lost so much for so little in return.

CHAPTER TWENTY-THREE
"Shinnecock Sachem's Daughter" Marries Wamapanog Son

Shinnecock Sachem, Nowedonah and Sabra's daughter, Jerusha married Charles Waters, they my eighth Great Grandparents.

Charles was of Wampanoag, decent, from his Mother, Mary-Mary. She the sister of Chief Sachem, Massasoit of the Wampanoag tribe of Rhode Island.

"Wampanoag", which means; "People of first light".

Charles' Father, Evans Waters, came over from York England in the early 16th century and landed in Virginia.

He traveled to the upper hills of Connecticut and to Rhode Island.

Evans' marriage of convenience to Mary-Mary (English name Margaret), Enabled him to obtain land grants, concerning Indian lands.

Evans with Chief Uncas of the Mohegan's was involved in a land patent and obtained one hundred acres in Virginia.

Evans and Mary-Mary had five children together. Three sons, Charles, David & Solomon and two daughters Savory and Abigail Waters. In the year 1630, Mary-Mary left Rhode Island with her three sons.

They landed in Stratford Connecticut. Upon a site called "Fresh Pond" which was the largest Cupheag Indian Village in Stratford. It extended from "Mac's Harbor" along "Shell Keep Point".

Mary-Mary settled on the "Little Neck" higher ground. (Little Neck today is known as the Sewage Disposal Plant, along the bank of the river, where the Avco Plant is now located)

This was all Indian villages and family clan group campsites. The "Little Neck" higher ground was a long narrow strip of upland to the southward of Mac's Harbor", lying between the Housatonic River, meaning; "Land beyond the mountain" on the east and Little Neck Creek on the west.

The shores of this sheltered inlet were called a Cupheag by a Paugusset Indian called Okenuck. He lived upon the Cupheag and was the son of Sachem Ansantaway, the Paugusset's Great Sachem.

They were an unwarlike and docile people, bullied by the Mohegans to the north and by the Pequots to the east.

In the year 1636 Mary-Mary's brother, Chief Massasoit kept the Wampanoags out of the first major Indian-White conflict in New England, which resulted in the near destruction of the Pequots.

So, on account of the troubling conditions in New England, it was not safe for my Wampanoag Ancestors to stay on the Little Neck higher ground.

So they left the New England area and came to what they called Little Neck. ("Men-haden-ock"). The namesake of their old home at Stratford Connecticut.

CHAPTER TWENTY-FOUR
"Men-haden-ock" Madnan's Neck

Men-haden-ock, meaning; "Place of Fish" which was shortened to "Madnan's Neck", was divided into two "Necks", Little Neck and Great Neck.

This land was once the land of the Matinecock Indians. They were members of the Algonquin Nation, of the Turkey and Turtle Clan. An Algonquin speaking people with a Lenni –Lenape dialect.

The Matinecocks, meaning; "People of the Hilly Land" were a peaceful people. They were one of the most prominent Chieftaincies on the North Shore.

Their territory extended all the way from Flushing Bay, on the west, to the Nissequogue River, at Smithtown, and south to the center of the Island.

They were famous for manufacturing wampum, Longhouses and the beautiful singing voices of their women.

In the 1600's the Matinecock tribe was under the leadership of a Chief.

Chief Tackapusha was the Great Chief of the Matinecock. He was the son of Agagonmon, also known as "One Eye" or Whitneyman, the Grand Sachem of lower New York State. Tackapusha had five siblings. Chepercowaw (The "Chipouse" family's ancestor) Conjamin, Samos, Oroway and Rumsuck.

Tackapusha stood eight feet tall as did his Brother Rumsuck. Tackapusha married and had two sons, Opposum and Asharoken.

Asharoken later became Matinecock Sachem and the Father of Catoneras.

Tackapusha feared that his people would be crushed by the Dutch Settlers, so he formed an alliance with the Sachems from other Indian Bands of the region to represent the Algonquin's at negotiations with the Dutch.

This action by Tackapusha helped make him one of the two most powerful Algonquin Leaders on Long Island, the other being Wyandanch.

CHAPTER TWENTY-FIVE

"Matinecock Indians" Of (Madnan's Neck)

The Matinecocks were a noble people who had lived in harmony with nature for over a thousand years on Long Island's north shore.

The English and Dutch Settlers put down roots on Little Neck Bay in the 1640s.

They had difficulty with the Indians over ownership. The Indians felt that they bartered some land to the southward but not to the northward.

The Matinecock were willing to share the land with the settlers from Europe, but the settlers wanted it all.

There was a meeting between the Indians and white Settlers. Sachem Tackapousha argued that the Northern Necks of their lands was Indian land before the White man came and never been sold to them.

The White man however, claimed that the Chief himself had sold Little Neck (Madnan's Neck) to them for one hundred and twenty pounds.

The simple ways of the Matinecock were no match for the power of the new Settlers.

Sadly the Indians who were ignorant of the White man's greed for land fell prey to it and what was once theirs was lost forever. In 1656, Englishman, Thomas Hicks brought the Matinecocks a deadly blow.

He led a band of armed White men with muskets against the Indians and drove them from their last settlement and fishing grounds on Little Neck Bay. This last pitched battle was fought on the present site of the Little Neck Douglaston Library, at Marathon Parkway and Northern Boulevard.

Here the Matinecock Warriors faced the deadly guns of the White man and here the Indians were slaughtered. Some were able to escape to Connecticut by way of the Long Island Sound, while a few others fled to the south eastern section of the Island.

Quakers took in most of the women and children and raised them as members of their families. They attacked until only the women and children and a few elderly men were all that remained, of what was once the wealthiest of all Long Island Tribes.

Thomas Hicks seized their North Shore Islands for himself. Decimated over the years by white man's diseases against which they had no immunity, the Indian population rapidly decreased.

With the loss of their land, the remaining Matinecocks moved to join with Poospatuck, Shinnecock And the Montauketts, who by the late 1600s had negotiated some of their own lands, which later became Reservations.

The Matinecocks that chose to stay on their ancestral land settled within small hamlets near the sites of their earlier villages and sought work on the new English plantations.

CHAPTER TWENTY-SIX

"Mary Mary" Waters Wampanoag Squaw

But not all the Indians are gone from the Little Neck area. Mary-Mary who had departed the Little Neck higher ground in Stratford Connecticut in 1636 had settled in Madnan's Neck with one of her sons, Charles Waters.

Charles went out to the Shinnecock Indian Reservation and married Jerusha Lott, the only daughter of Shinnecock Grand Sachem, Nowedonah and Sabra "Sybel" Lott.

Charles & Jerusha's marriage early in the century settled effectually the feud which for a long time – hundreds of years, in fact – kept the Narragansetts and the Montauketts on the warpath.

At that time the whole eastern end of Long Island belonged to the Montauketts and according to the original grant, "As long as there remains a drop of Montauk blood in the veins of living man that land belongs to them still."

Charles and Jerusha resided upon both, Shinnecock and the Poospatuck Indian Reservations before returning to Madnan's Neck, to the family's homestead property.

They settled upon Madnan's Neck for Charles' Father, Evans was granted a Land Grant by the English Sovereign in the early 1600s.

Charles built the original Waters' home. A two story colonial dwelling, with one room on each floor. With a large oven outside and a well dug out in front.

The Waters' home, one of the landmarks on the north shore, has since been occupied by the family.

On March 12th, 1644, Charles II wrote a new patent for his brother James, the Duke of York, incorporating Long Island into the Colony of New York.

It was decided that Long Island would be part of New York rather than Connecticut. This news was not received favorably by East Enders.

The town now had laws against offenses such as lying and drunkenness.

For lying, the penalty was five shillings or five hours in the stocks.

For drunkenness, ten shillings for the first offense, twenty for the second, and thirty for the third offense. Public Punishment for crimes was now common.

There was also a law prohibiting the sale of articles of war or liquor to the Indians.

The Land Grants continued to spread around the Waters Native family like nets, from 1636-1666.

But the Indian family felt no need at any time to leave the land that had once been the birth right of their Race.

For, Sachem Nowedonah's Grandson married and resided upon the Waters' homestead property. His own son married a Montaukett Squaw.

The Great Grandson of Sachem Nowedonah was, Charles Waters, he was born in the year 1762.

Charles married Jerusha "Locke" Larkee, she a Montaukett Squaw.

CHAPTER TWENTY-SEVEN
"My Fifth Great Grandparents"

Jerusha's Father was John Locke; her Mother was Sibby Larkin, a Montaukett Squaw of Montauk Point.

Sibby, while gathering firewood one day from her forest, came upon a Negro boy. A Fugitive from a ship that brought Africans from their coasts, to be sold within these United States had landed at Montauk Point.

Sibby led the boy to her wigwam, named him "Solomon" Hubbs and as a chore-boy for her family: he grew up among the Indians and was loved by all of them.

Jerusha's sister, Sylvia grew up and married their Solomon. They settled with Jerusha and her family upon the family's homestead in Madnan's Neck.

Here is where the two sisters, Jerusha Waters and Sylvia Hubbs raised their families.

After the Revolutionary War, so put an end to the English Land Grants.

It is recorded in the 1808 Queens County Records, Sylvia Hubbs purchased from Cornelius Van Wyck, a few acres on Hempstead Plain, for an abiding place at Old South Landing, in Little Neck, Long Island. (Madnan's Neck).

Sylvia had to buy back their ancestral land!

Sylvia Hubbs was a School Teacher, whom taught class in her attic on Hempstead Plain. Her sister, Jerusha was a maid for Thomas Hicks (Milord Hicks, as he was called then).The two sisters had children that wed.

Sylvia's daughter, Mary Hubbs married James Waters, son of Jerusha...

CHAPTER TWENTY-EIGHT
"James Waters" & Mary Hubbs

My Fourth Great Grandparents, James and Mary resided upon the family's homestead property. The parcel of land in which Sylvia, had to buy back from Cornelius Van Wyck of Flushing.

The ten acres were purchased for the sum of three hundred seventy-five dollars. A portion of this land was laid aside by Sylvia in about 1810 as the family's private Indian Burial Ground.

Sylvia's daughter, Mary Hubbs Waters inherited the parcel of land (includes the cemetery) from her Mother. The Deed (according to the records at the Queens Clerk's Office) details the boundaries of this piece of property, which shows it to be the piece on the north side of Northern Blvd. and the west side of Little Neck Parkway.

Mary's husband, James Waters passed away at the early age of twenty-six, leaving a young wife and four children, John, Charles, Elisha and Mary.

When their Mother passed away the three surviving Waters children inherited the property, John, Charles, and Mary.

CHAPTER TWENTY-NINE

"The Waters / Davis" Family Feud begins

After the death of Sylvia, her children began to argue and fight with each other over the homestead property.

In the 1800s Mary Waters had passed away, and left behind her ten minor children.

Her brothers, Charles and John then began to petition the removal of the minor Davis children from the homestead property, their sister's children.

For Charles had taken his own brother and sister to court, for the division of their property.

By the year 1900, the partition suit was settled.

John became owner of the corner lot with the house.

The corner lot was deemed more valuable than the others and therefore John was ordered to pay three hundred dollars to Charles who voluntarily took the plot surrounding the burying ground and two hundred dollars was to go to Mary who had taken the plot in back of that allotted to Charles before her death.

Charles' home was built on the parcel of land at a point marked by a locust post, on the Northwesterly corner of land, on Cornell Lane. Here he resided with his Wife, Jane Davis. (This has since been torn down).

Mary had resided in the old cottage on the back property of her brother Charles, with her husband, Joseph Davis.

Sadly, upon the deaths of their parents, Joseph Davis and Mary Waters, Sylvia, James, Mary, Joseph, Emma, Jesse, Dan, Sarah and Thomas Davis had to leave their home on the family's homestead property.

The siblings scattered. Some believe Dan went to Connecticut, the other Davis siblings, went to live with family members. They went out to the Shinnecock Reservation and other parts of the Island.

Jesse Davis, was the last family owner of The eastern boundary of land that was two hundred sixty and forty-five one hundredth feet from Old House Landing Road.

Thus began the family feud of the Davis children and their Uncles, Charles and John Waters.

Which also brought on in that same year, the family feud between the Waters and Davis families, over a twelve foot wide Right Away, a boundary of land between the two homesteads that led out to Old House Landing Road.

CHAPTER THIRTY

"My Third Great Grandfather"
John Mapevanisto Waters

John Mapevanisto Waters (Chief John) the brother of Charles and Mary Waters had inherited his birthplace, the original Waters' home.

His Grandfather, Charles, came here and built the colonial dwelling in the 1600s, on what was then Broadway.

Seventy years later an addition was being built but progress slowed because while the carpenters were at work on the building, they had to give their services to the American Army. But the largest end of the house was completed after.

The house had low ceilings and wide fireplaces. The shingles, handmade were fastened with wrought iron nails. The furniture was more antique than the colonial architecture of the building.

Outside in front of the house, a large oven stood for cooking and a well was near by.

The old well had a pole swung over it, on which was hung a rope to pull the bucket of water up. The well was doing the duty as the water supply for the family.

John Waters married Elizabeth Townsend, a Matinecock/ Montaukett Squaw from Southold Long Island. She was the daughter of Benjamin Townsend and Isabelle Seamen.

Elizabeth is the sister of Hannah Townsend Chisholm, the once owner of Lake Success, Long Island.

John and Elizabeth raised thirteen children. Maria, Elyahiana (Oney), Hannah, Bertha, Susan, Solomon, Sylvia, Solomon ll, John, James, Sidney, Jeffry and Isaac (Ike) Waters all in their shingled house that once sat among the giant honey locusts and oak trees that framed an emerald green lawn.

This was often the setting for an October celebration of the Harvest Season.

Here Blackfoot, Unkechaug, Apache, Powhatan, Matinecock, Penobscot and Cherokee joined with the Miccosukee – Seminoles, Narragansett and the Sioux all gathered together and listened to the words of the Medicine Man.

John liked to reminiscence of the bygone days. It was interesting as his home and ancestry, which he loved to recount.

My third Great Grandfather's memories of the Revolutionary incidents were centered on the doings of a member of his family, called Elijah. Who lived with the Schenck family in Dutch Hollow (Manhasset).

The British raided the Country for provisions and horses. Elijah was left in charge of the farm, as his "Master" had fled from the British

Soldiers. Elijah deserted to the enemy, sold a pair of horses to an English Officer left Dutch Hollow with the Army and was never heard of after. John, at the time, heard of an Indian family named Waters living in Pennsylvania. Who had formally been in Long Island and who proved to be descendants of the runaway Elijah.

John's Grandmother Jerusha was the Maid in the family. She would tell John, many stories of the baronial style of living, of Milford Hicks (Thomas Hicks). How he was in the colonial days, Lord of the extensive manor of Little Neck.

In February of 1903 John M. Waters passed away. He was interred along side his Wife, Elizabeth Townsend Waters in the family's private Indian Burial Ground.

As to this very day, both my third Great Grandfather and Grandmother are among the missing. For the City (bearing the expense) dug up the Indian Burial Ground, to widen Northern Blvd.

When my ancestors were transferred to Zion Church-yard cemetery in Douglaston, to be re-interred, John and Elizabeth were not accounted for. They along with other ancestors are "Amongst the Missing".

CHAPTER THIRTY-ONE
"Chief James Edward" Wild Pigeon Waters

John's son, James, was one of thirteen children. He was born in the house of his Father in the year 1873.

James was a licensed second grade Teacher but was employed as a clerk in the General Post Office in Manhattan. He was a faithful and competent worker.

He was also a member of the Flushing Historical Society and was regarded as an authority upon local History. For in his time, for some several years, he was collecting data for a book of memoirs he was writing.

James was a fantastic character, he an interpreter of Indian dialects.

He became a member of the Montaukett Tribal Council in the year 1914. (He was also Sachem of the Matinecock Tribe). He became actively involved in all things concerning his people. He was intelligent, forceful and experienced in Indian Affairs.

James brought to the tribe, support and enthusiasm, in which they needed. Many Algonquin families on Long Island knew and respected him. James developed a membership roll of five hundred-six contributors.

On August 31st, 1916, at the annual meeting in Sag Harbor, James was now identified as the Chief of the tribal council. He was fighting for the Montauketts land and their tribal status. He fought to give the Montauketts a modern Political structure. Delegating for the tribe, he fought to show cause, the Montauketts were not extinct.

He may have been a bit to aggressive for some, but the defeats and long delays however, cost James the support from the tribe. In the year 1923 the council rejected James as Chief.

In the summer of 1924, James Waters did not take his removal from office gracefully. He had sued Allen Cuffee (Whom had resigned as Sachem) for the tribal records.

Mr. Cuffee had to turn the records over, for the Judge agreed with Mr. Waters. As for what the case stated we do not know for sure. The records are "missing".

James Water's home had eventually stood empty. Until the City took it over in the year 1944 for non-payment of back taxes and knocked it down.

With the ruin of the original Waters home, family papers, documents etc. were lost.

The last three years of James' life were devoted to a struggle to save his family's Indian Burial Ground, which was located on the side of his three acre home. (Northern Blvd). The Burial ground was scheduled to be moved to accommodate the widening of the street.

Chief James Wild Pigeon's opposition to the removal of the bodies resulted in the delay in the widening of Northern Blvd. in the section about the cemetery.

Chief Wild Pigeon was the last of the Sachems adhering to the ancient traditions of his Fathers.

He declared the ground in which his people were buried was sacred and he threatened to unearth the tomahawk buried by his ancestors the Narragansett, to commemorate their refusal to participate in King Philips War.

He recited the legend of his ancestors coming to "Seawanhaka" (Long Island) many moons ago, before the coming of the White Settler. He said, Little Neck Cemetery had been the burial ground of the heroic Indians and he would not have their remains disturbed.

Tradition has it, that some of the graves were then, almost three hundred years old. Their occupants saw the ancient glory of the Montauketts when they lorded over the other Long Island Tribes and quite probably, fought in the last great war of the people when riddled by pestilence and harried by the arrows and war clubs of the Narragansetts.

They were driven westward almost the whole length of their domain to seek shelter with the whites.

James Wild Pigeon heir to heroic tradition was resolved to defend the burial ground of his ancestors from encroachment. It was his wish to be buried there when he died.

He fought the white man with the weapons of the whites. He went to court to save the graves of his Fathers'. The court decided against him but directed that the bodies be exhumed and buried elsewhere.

James stated: "Even in death the Indian must move on at the command of the whites". His hope that his body might lie where the Warriors of his race first had been interred was shattered.

He was a victim of a long and losing struggle against the whites as surely as though he had been struck down by a bullet. He had put his whole heart into this fight to save the ancient Indian Burial Ground, which the City had condemned for the widening of the thoroughfare.

So, another of the many last stands of the Red Man in the United States was discovered here and as usual, it was a losing struggle for the Indians.

In a poison ivy patch directly in the path of the road-widening project, lies a score or more graves. They contained the bodies of Narragansett Indians who came to Long Island when it was wild and untilled.

James believed others should have helped him protect the graveyard. He said, white people were buried there too. If so, the names and circumstances of the dead long have been worn away from most of the headstones.

The widening of the road had enhanced the value of James' property. Its value had been estimated as high as $200.000 (at that time).

James and his sisters Oney and Sue Waters declined to listen to purchase overtures made by Real Estate Men. Over the protests of Real Estate agents in this part of Long Island, the Waters continued to live in a cottage across the street from the graveyard. The cabin and its surrounding plot of ground would sell for $175.000, estimated.

There were buyers but James would not sanction the sale and without his sanction his sisters would not sell.

For James and his sisters, there was no temptation in the prospect of plenty and comfort in exchange for poverty and discomfort. It would be an easy matter to achieve the transformation by selling their Homestead.

The graveyard had to be sold, to meet demands of road makers. But James Wild Pigeon Waters and his sisters, who took in washing for their livelihood, would not sell.

James had suffered from a heart attack. He was taken home and on September 3rd, 1927, shortly before five AM James E. Waters passed away. Both his sisters bleakly agreed James died at home, on Old House Landing Road. They stated: heart disease as the cause of death.

He was survived by his two sisters, Oney and Sue Waters, a brother, John Waters and his only child a daughter, Belinda Waters.

After his death, James' two sisters, took up the fight to bar the City from widening Northern Blvd. on the grounds that the improvement would run through the family burial ground.

But the old Indian Burial Ground gave way to the City in 1931 to the widening of Northern Blvd. in Little Neck.

The Waters had to give up a thirteen foot strip along Northern Blvd. on the side of their three acre home.

It was finally arranged that a plot purchased in Zion Churchyard in Douglaston was the place the bones of the buried Indians would be placed.

Objecting, were the two sisters, Oney and Sue. It was abhorrent to them to see the bones of their ancestors desecrated and scattered to the four winds.

After James Wild Pigeon's death, the corporation counsel obtained permission to remove the bodies.

Ironically, James Waters' wish to be buried with his ancestors was finally realized four years after his death.

With the City bearing the expense, they removed the ancestral remains and transferred them to Zion Church-yard cemetery in Douglaston, along side Chief James Edward "Wild Pigeon" Waters.

CHAPTER THIRTY-TWO

"The Waters Sisters" Oney & Sue

In the year 1936 Susan and Oney Waters had a public unveiling of a monument they purchased and dedicated. The monument is a split boulder with an oak tree growing between its sides, to symbolize the victory of life over death. It was unveiled in Zion Church-yard where their family members are buried.

On the boulder, the inscription reads: "Here Rest the Last of the Matinecoc".

The sisters lived on their land until their deaths. Miss Susan Waters died on April 15th, 1941. She left her sister Oney Waters a large bequest.

Miss Oney Waters lived alone since her sister's death. She insisted on living in the small unpainted house where she was born, despite the large inheritance left to her by her sister. She said she was staying until she died.

Oney resided in the little old fashioned house, lighted by oil lamps and heated by pot stoves in every room. Her difference to progress and the paleface way of living stemmed directly from her Narragansett forefathers

Oney Waters passed away in 1944 at the age of ninety-two. Her death left the house vacant. The new owners under the supervision of the Department of Health began to clear the land for "improvements". They were required to excavate to a depth of ten feet. They found at three cubic feet, bones and some evidence of disintegrated caskets. This material was later deposited in the Waters' plot in Zion Cemetery.

The City paid a visit to the members of the Waters' family who continued living on a site adjacent to the cemetery grounds; they were surprised to find the then 84 year old John Waters, brother of James Wild Pigeon Waters! And he, like his brother, having a high consciousness of pride in his ancestry.

CHAPTER THIRTY-THREE

"Chief Sachem" John H. Standing Waters

John, born in the house of his Father and Grandfather in the year 1863 was a man of extraordinary intelligence.

Except for a sojourn of several years in Connecticut, he has lived all his life in Little Neck. Making his living until his 80s by hunting, fishing and landscape gardening. He often clammed in Little Neck Bay and other Long Island waters.

John Waters' interests in Indian Affairs were many. He kept his family ties with the Narragansetts. He was affiliated with the sons and daughters of the first Americans of Rhode Island with the Narragansetts. He and his children were members of the Narragansett Tribe of Rhode Island.

John became a member of the Narragansett tribe, December 13th, 1923. His Daughter Maidie "Princess Heather Flower" became a member on October 28th, 1929 and his Son, LaRocque "Little Wolf" on October 30th, 1929. John and his children were also lifetime members of the United Association of the American Indians.

They would take the bus up every year, with their cousins, to attend the Narragansett Pow wow. There they would gather with their friends and family. They attended yearly until 1972-73.

John wanted to carry on his brother's dream of reorganizing the Matinecock tribe. For after the death of James E. "Wild Pigeon" Waters in the year 1927, the Matinecock Tribe dissolved and had lain dormant.

In 1958 two Matinecock sisters, Ann Harding Murdock (Princess Sun Tama) and Lila Elizabeth Harding (Princess Brown Thrush) organized an informal longhouse.

So, on May 8th, 1958 the Matinecock Indians and an overflow crowd of more than three hundred well wishers and descendants of the original tribe gathered as the tribal flame was re-lit as Chief John H. Standing Waters was installed as Senior Chieftain of the tribe.

The service was held at the Zion Episcopal Church in Douglaston.

Princess Sun Tama was voted in as spokesperson in all matters pertaining to the tribe.

She was the driving force of the re-organization of the Matinecock tribe. Princess Sun Tama stated: Their tribe had been sleeping quietly for many, many years. It was time to unite again for the good of the tribe.

The first action of the reactivated tribe was notifying the North American Indian Council that the Matinecock exist as a unified tribe once again.

Chief John Standing Waters' son, Little Wolf (LaRocque Waters) was a Medicine Man and his daughter Princess Heather Flower (Maidie Waters) tribal secretary of the Matinecock tribe.

Sun Tama fought the City, State and Federal Government on tribal territorial claims, to give her Matinecock people the right to be what they want to be.

John H. "Standing" Waters, Chieftain of the Matinecock Indians of Long Island, passed away at the age of one hundred-two years, on Friday, June 4th, 1965 at Long Island Jewish Hospital, New Hyde Park, after a brief illness.

He was the first member of the family to trace our ancestry to Evans Waters, who came to America from England in the early 17th century and found he married Mary-Mary, sister of Sachem Massasoit of the Wampanoag tribe of Rhode Island.

John was laid to rest beside his wife Maidie Waters. She had passed away six years prior. Both are interred at Nassau Knolls Cemetery.

After the death of the Senior Chieftain and the death of the Charismatic leader, Ann Harding Murdock (Princess Sun Tama) in 1969, tribal leadership has been a recurrent problem.

The Matinecock Longhouse of Long Island, a formal organization was chartered by the State of New York, in 1985 but it is now inactive, having fallen to disagreements and lack of spirit.

At present, the tribe has a Chief but many Matinecock followers reject his authority.

But not all the Indians have become dispirited. My family, whose descendants are those who resided here upon the shores of Little Neck since the 1600s, cling steadfast to their Native identity.

Our family lineage goes back to the Narragansetts of 1432, the Montauketts of 1551 and the Shinnecock of 1573. We also have blood ties to the Wampanoags of 1650 and the Pequots of 1456.

Upon the deaths of John's children, Maidie in 1976 and LaRocque in 1998, the community lost a link with its glorious beginnings.

At present time we still have members of our family living in Little Neck.

Chief John Standing Waters Grandson, LaRocque Mongotucksee Waters, is one of the last direct descendants of the Waters family clan, a cousin to me. He today, along with his family resides in one of the last two original Waters' homesteads.

CHAPTER THIRTY-FOUR
"Solomon Jefferies Waters"

The other Indian family, next door are Great Grandchildren of Chief John's brother, Solomon Jefferies Waters.

My Great, Great Grandfather, Solomon, a Montaukett tribal member, was born in 1859 and he grew up on the Waters' homestead property with his twelve brothers and sisters.

Solomon was a laborer at the age of nineteen. He married my Great, Great Grandmother; Mary Elizabeth Treadwell on December 2nd, 1885.Solomon was then twenty-five years old. Together he and Mary had seven children, Benjamin, Harrison "Harry", John Starbuck, Maria "Patsy", Bertha "Bert", Adeline and Serena "Rene".

Solomon also raised his Wife's son an Unkechaug Indian whose name was Gil Treadwell.

In the year 1901 Solomon built their home on the Waters family's homestead property. But sadly, Mary at the age of thirty-two passed away suddenly of that same year.

Solomon married again, to Sarah and she helped raise the Waters children. They all resided in their small home on Cornell Lane, in Little Neck.

Solomon took up work with the Village BlackSmith, which was doing business on Little Neck Parkway, south of Northern Boulevard. Here Solomon worked with his step son, Gil Treadwell.

Solomon Jefferies Waters passed away in 1925. He had a Native American Burial and was laid to rest in his Traditional Native Blanket, alongside his siblings in Zion's Church-yard Cemetery in Douglaston.

Solomon's daughter, Bertha (Aunt Bert) was born February 16th, 1897. She met and married her husband Howard Williams, in Little Neck.

They moved to Rhode Island and resided at: 22 Carrington Avenue in Providence Rhode Island. Here they lived through the forties and fifties.

The Waters clan would meet here and have family gatherings at Rodger Williams Park and attend the Narragansett Tribal meetings, and Pow wows.

Sadly, Aunt Bert & Uncle Howard's home suffered a fatal house fire. They moved into an apartment on the back property of their old home for a period of time.

They, then decided to move back home to Little Neck, to the Waters' family homestead.

Uncle Howard passed away shortly thereafter, and Aunt Bert stayed in her Father's house until her death in March of 1982.

Solomon Waters' step son, Gil Treadwell had become of age and he moved to the Poospatuck Indian Reservation, to live with his believed to be Father, Chief of the Reservation, Walter Treadwell.

Part Three

The Poospatuck Revervation
Unkechaug Nation

(Dedicated to Virginia Davis Miller)

Brookhaven: "The Manor of St. George"

(Named after England's King George)

Moriches, Center Moriches, East Moriches:

Meritche

Merquices

Maritches

Marigies

Meritces

Moritches

Muriches

Moricha

Poospatuck; "Where the Waters Meet"

Unkechaug; "People from Beyond the Hill"

Although Poospatuck is sometimes used interchangeably with Unkechaug, Poospatuck is a place name and Unkechaug is the tribal name.

The Poospatuck initially constituted one of the numerous American villages linked by kinship to a confederacy that stretched across Long Island and southern New England.

These relationships still connect the Poospatucks, Montauketts, Shinnecock, the Mohegan, Narragansett, Pequot and Wampanoags.

CHAPTER THIRTY-FIVE

"The Poospatuck Indian Reservation"

In the eastern part of Mastic and the northern part of Moriches bordering on the East Bay is the Poospatuck Indian Reservation.

At one time, it was cut up by numerous hills and valleys. It was covered with a rank growth of shrub and tall prairie grass.

On the eastern side of the Reservation was "Flint Hill". So called on account of the flint stones which were abound there.

Much has been written about the Long Island Indians, where many thousands of Red Men once lived.

CHAPTER THIRTY-SIX

"The Unkechaug Indian"

The Unkechaug dwelled along the coast, rivers and streams. Their village was established in a slash and burn clearing.

Their dwellings, called wigwams, were made from saplings Joined together and lashed at the top. The wigwam was then covered with skin or clay. They were different in size and shapes

Some were domed shaped structures from ten to twenty feet in diameter, covered with grass. The clay was used at the tops of the dwellings to prevent them from burning when fires were lit inside. The vents allowed smoke and heat to escape.

Single family wigwams were circular, where a multiple dwelling was long and cylindrical.

They resided in a circle with their doors facing to the east.

The tribe lived fairly prosperly. Chiefly they were Hunters and Fishermen.

Game was rather plentiful on the island. The Unkechaug hunted deer, bear, raccoon, turkey, quail, partridge, goose and duck. Also eaten was, otter, elk, and muskrat.

Seafood was also plentiful. From the sea they ate many forms of fish.

Such as clams, oysters, mussels, turtles, eels, crab, lobster and whales. The Indians were expert Fishermen, equally adept with bows and arrows or simple hook/string methods of catching fish.

They hunted whales in canoes and always used the entire whale, including whale oil for their lamps, which they burned in large clam shells.

The Unkechaugs would boil the blubber and mix the oil with their corn and beans, or they would rub the oil into animal hides as a preservative.

Large game was shot with bow and arrows while smaller game were snared or trapped.

The Unkechaug would do their cooking in a communal roasting pit. Here they would prepare their wild game. They would also use this shallow pit for steaming their various seafood.

The women did all of the farm work by hand or with crude Implements, made by hand. They raised corn, beans, pumpkins, squash, cucumbers and tobacco.

The raising of the tobacco was the only farm work the men did.

The average Unkechaug male was tall, slender, strong and muscular. The women were just the opposite. Short, slim but with good bone structure and capable of hard work and bearing pain.

The Unkechaug had the capacity to cure. They had many remedies for truly life threatening health problems, as well as for simple cuts and burns.

Herbs and roots were used before contact with the Europeans. Sassafras helped enable the body to withstand high temperatures. Sap of milkweed was a good antiseptic. Also, the sap from white pine and cherry trees made a good syrup for coughs.

CHAPTER THIRTY-SEVEN
"Meetings & Celebrations"

The Unkechaug would get together with their relations, the Montauketts and the Shinnecock.

Their celebrations carried down through hundreds of years. For the Harvest of the Corn celebration all the clans would gather. They would eat, dance and socialize. Many young couples met and married through these celebrations.

Since before the coming of the white man, the June Meeting Day was and still is an annual event of great important to the Poospatuck tribe.

CHAPTER THIRTY-EIGHT
"The European Settlers Arrival"

The earliest inhabitants of the Moriches area were the Native Americans. This land was all theirs before the Europeans arrived.

Moriches was part of the area to become Brookhaven town.

The town of Brookhaven is the largest on Long Island and extends across the island from the Sound to the ocean and is about twenty miles long, east and west. The main village was located in Mastic.

The Indians living in Mastic-Moriches are the Unkechaug, which means: "People from Beyond the Hill". They had a population, once which numbered twenty thousand.

When the Europeans landed on the east end of Long Island in October of 1640, there was a struggle for it's ownership.

A party of six men, John Scudder, John Swezie, Jonathan Porter, Roger Chester and Thomas Charles came from the colonies of New England.

The sixth man, Thomas Mabbs belonged to Southold, Long Island. He accompanied the others as being a man of experience in dealing with the Natives.

They landed on the shores of the beautiful bays and coves of Setauket. Meaning; "Land at the Mouth of the Creek", home of the Setauket Indians, they a most friendly and peaceful people.

This small English lot had at first settled in Lynn Massachusetts then continued to the South Fork of Long Island.

These English Farmers who lived near the sea must have found this place quite suitable and probably surprisingly milder than the land they left in either England or Lynn Massachusetts.

The party had with them the usual collection of coats, hatchets, powder, knives and the like with which to do a land deal with the Indians.

The English Settlers main business was agriculture. They made a deal with the Setauket Chief, Sachem, Warawasen "Warawakmy" for thirty square miles extending from Stony Brook to Port Jefferson.

The island then became linked with the rest of the country!

The Settler soon began to explore the south side and discovered large meadows of salt hay and grass which could be harvested for their cattle.........

CHAPTER THIRTY-NINE
"Mastic"

The Indians had no experience with land deals and at the time could not comprehend the true meaning of these transactions.

For starting in the year 1664, Unkechaug Sachem Tabacus started selling the land owned by the Unkechaug. Tracts of land from South Haven to Bellport, and north to the middle of the island. Also, all the land west of this to the Islip line.

The Unkechaug were trusting people. They believed the land was there for everyone to use. When all the buying of the land was going on, the Unkechaug still thought they would be able to hunt, fish and live where they wanted to, just as they had always done.

But instead, the Settlers mowed down the Unkechaug's fields, for fodder for their cattle and horses. They damned their streams and took the shallow ones and made them into roads.

Gone were the Native's woodlands, for the Settlers needed housing and food. Saw mills were set up to saw the trees into lumber for houses and millstones were used to grind corn and wheat grown for their food.

Small hamlets sprung up at the apex of roads and rivers. Gone were the Unkechaug's Rolling Meadows and Woodlands, for they gave way to farms and villages.

The Native Americans roamed the shores for hundreds of years, farming, fishing and hunting. But it took the English barely two generations after landing on Long Island in 1640 to make Mastic their own.

CHAPTER FORTY

"Col. William "Tangier" Smith"

Just prior to the loss of all their land, five Unkechaug men went to visit the then Governor Fletcher. They asked the Governor to stop his people from taking their land.

But the Governor, in order to satisfy a debt owed to the Government for Military services rendered, gave Col. William "Tangier" Smith along with his brothers a patent of land each. This was called the "Moriches Patent".

Given was the tract of land at Mastic River and extending north to the middle of the island. Col. Smith then subdivided the land to the Floyd Family.

Thus, taking away land that belonged to the Unkechaug. With the loss of their land, the Unkechaug had no place to go.

One day while hunting on his estate, Col. Smith found The small bedraggled tribe of Indians, eating what they found to survive.

They explained to Col. Smith they had nowhere to go, that all their land had been taken by the white man. These remnants of the Unkechaugs were living in a swampy tract near present day Mastic.

So, in that year, of 1700, Col. Smith gave the Unkechaug Indians the right to use and raise crops on a one hundred seventy-five acre of land, on the Mastic River.

The deed signed to the Unkechaug stated:

"The Poospatucks and all their children and all their children's children unto posterity, shall have rights to this land forever, so long as Indian Blood, no matter how little, ran through their veins".

Col. Smith granted the Unkechaug the 175 acres near the banks of the Forge River "in Perpetuity". But within a generation, the Smith family began to sell off chunks of this "175 Perpetuity", which evidently lost its meaning quickly to their wealthy neighbors, the Floyds. Soon, the Floyd's had all but 60 acres of the original 175.

CHAPTER FORTY-ONE

"Peter John Cuffee"

My seventh Great Grandfather was Peter John Cuffee. He was born at the Hay Ground in the Parish of Bridgehampton, in South Hampton, in the year 1712. He was a Shinnecock Indian.

Peter John converted to Christianity during the time when most churches in this country were trying to get a foot hold in the colonies.

He took up residence in St. George's Manor, (Moriches) where he owned property. Peter John had excellent ability as a Speaker, Organizer and Leader. He worked among the Indians as far west as Islip.

He founded a church at Wading River and Poospatuck. Although his plan was to establish a church at Canoe Place, it was not accomplished until his Grandson and successor Paul Cuffee was brought into the Ministry.

Peter John Cuffee lived to the advanced age of eighty-eight years and is buried on the Poospatuck Reservation.

CHAPTER FORTY-TWO

"Peter Paul Cuffee"

Peter Paul Cuffee like his Father, Peter John was active in the church. Although not a Minister, he was liked by all who knew him.

Peter Paul Cuffee is my sixth Great Grandfather, who married Jane Peters, a Shinnecock.

Jane Peters Cuffee was for many years a respected member of the Native Indian Church at Wading River. She was employed in the household of the family bearing the name "Hudson".

Jane was a devout, energetic and dignified woman.

CHAPTER FORTY-THREE

"Stephen Cuffee" Chief Cuffee

Peter and Jane had seven sons. Their forth son, Stephen Cuffee (Chief Cuffee) of the Poospatuck Reservation was born in the year 1761 just outside Bridgehampton. He is my fifth Great Grandfather and Brother of the Native Preacher, the Reverend Paul Cuffee.

Stephen married an Unkechaug Indian. Elizabeth Cuffee (Job) who was born in the year 1758. She was one of the last great Queens of Poospatuck.

Together she and Stephen had two children, Jesse and Joel Cuffee.

It wasn't a happy hunting ground in colonial times. For, Poospatuck men were sold in the slave trade. They were owned by white men just as they owned cattle, sheep and farm implements.

The Indians would work in the fields alongside their owners. Many of them worked their way into more skilled jobs as Craftsmen, such as Shoemakers, Blacksmiths and Woodworkers.

The women were taken as Concubines. They did outside work but more often were used as household servants.

Eventually there was intermarriage with runaway Slaves, who came to Long Island to find work with the general population.

(A 1679 New York State law forbid slavery of Native Americans, but it seemed to have continued illegally in some cases up to 1827).

The job market on Long Island could only afford Domestic or Farm Labor and paid very little.

Stephen was a Fisherman though whaling was so lucrative. For whale oil, blubber and whalebone were in great demand.

Unfortunately, whaling did take the men away from the Reservation for long periods of time and the women in order to hold the family together, worked. They were mostly in domestic service and were paid little.

Stephen Cuffee's son, Joel, my fourth Great Grandfather was a Shinnecock/Unkechaug Indian born in the year 1794. He was bound out to the Davis family's Peach farm, located in "Nonowatuck" (The Stream that dries up), Mount Sinai, Long Island, to help pay off the Cuffee family debt.

During the War of 1812, Stephen went aboard the USS Constitution and loaded the guns that helped nobly to defeat the British Frigate La Gueriere.

Stephen lost his life in battle while serving aboard The Constitution, fighting against the very Impressments forced upon him.

CHAPTER FORTY-FOUR

"Joel Cuffee Davis"

Joel Cuffee Davis married my fourth Great Grandmother, Sabra Waters, a Montaukett/Wampanoag Indian. She was born on Montauk Long Island, in the year 1804.

Joel and Sabra reside upon both the Shinnecock and the Poospatuck Indian Reservations. Joel, an Oysterman in the town of Brookhaven had ten children with Sabra.

Their children married and spread out upon Long Island. The siblings resided upon both Reservations, Manhasset and Little Neck Long Island.

One of their daughters, Martha Davis Maynes, was born in the same year that her Grandmother, Elizabeth Cuffee Job passed away, 1832.

Martha stood all of five feet three inches tall and strongly built. She became a great Queen on Poospatuck. After her second marriage, she went to live on the Shinnecock Reservation at Southampton but later returned to Poospatuck.

She became an active participant in all affairs of her little colony on Poospatuck.

CHAPTER FORTY-FIVE

"Joseph Davis" & Mary Waters

Martha's Brother, Joseph Davis is my third Great Grandfather.

He was born in Mastic, Long Island in the year 1832. He moved to Little Neck, Long Island and married his Montaukett/Wamapanoag cousin, Mary Waters.

They wed on March 14th, 1854 in the Parsonage of Zion Church in Douglaston, Queens.

Joseph and Mary resided upon the Waters' family homestead, on a share in which Mary inherited. They lived in the old cottage on the back property of her Brother, Charles Waters. Here they had raised ten children.

Joseph and Mary were interred in the family's private Indian burial ground. But in the year 1931 the Indian burial ground was dug up by the City of New York to widen Northern Blvd. Joseph and Mary's and many of our other Native ancestors final resting places are gone.

Joseph and Mary's family put up a long struggle and fight with the City of New York. Sadly, the Native American family lost their battle.

With the City bearing the expense, the Ancestral Remains were re-interred in Zion's Church-yard Cemetery. But, many were "lost". Until this day, they remain, not as unmarked graves, but lost souls.

CHAPTER FORTY-SIX

"William Davis" & Virginia Hunter

Joseph and Mary's son, William Davis, was my Great, Great Grandfather. He was born in the year 1856, and he married Virginia Hunter, a Matinecock/Shinnecock Indian.

She was the Granddaughter of Shinnecock Chief Jeremiah Hunter.

William and Virginia married on August 13th, 1878 in Zion Church of Douglaston, Queens and they settled in Manhasset, Long Island. William became a Sanitation Worker for a private company.

He and Virginia had seven children together. William Rosebud, who is the Grandfather of my cousin, Mollie Bluesky Boone, a daughter Mary Jane, son Charles, who is the Grandfather of, Poospatuck Chief, Harry Wallace a son Joseph and another daughter Bessie.

William Davis and Virginia Hunter also had a son by the name of Archibald Davis.

He was my Great Grandfather.

Archibald was four years old when his parents moved back to Little Neck, where they resided upon; 42-16 Clinton Street (250th Street).

My Great Grandparents Archibald & Adeline Waters remained in Little Neck and raised my Grandmother and her three brothers.

CHAPTER FORTY-SEVEN

"My Great Grandfather's brother" Charles Davis

Charles Davis, My Great Grandfather's brother was born in 1893. He moved to Flushing and married Lydia Davis. They raised thirteen children.

After Charles' death, Lydia moved to Little Neck. Their daughter, young Lydia was born in 1931. She is the Mother of Poospatuck Chief, Harry Wallace and she resides upon the Poospatuck Indian Reservation in Mastic, Long Island.

CHAPTER FORTY-EIGHT
"Poospatuck Chief" Harry B. Wallace

On April 5th, 1994, Harry Wallace was installed as Tribal Chief and he still reins today.

A tribal council was also installed. The council consists of seven members. The Chief, three Trustees, a Record Keeper, a Secretary and a Wampum Keeper.

Decisions according to the Chief are usually made consensus after lengthy discussions.

Chief Wallace deserves much praise for he has taken This Indian Reservation from: Lacking modern conveniences like, telephones and central heating. Also, polluted water wells and no fire hydrants.

To: Getting the Reservation homes hooked up to the county water system, having their roads and homes repaired and having their street lights turned on.

He also raised funds, to hire a cleaning crew which keeps the Reservation's grounds and their burial grounds clean.

Chief Wallace has most importantly, encouraged the revival of community gatherings and celebrations. These programs helped to stabilize and strengthen the community. This changed attitudes among the Unkechaug people and gave them more pride in their community.

This has placed an emphasis on reaffirming their Indian heritage and asserting their Tribal Sovereignty.

This Unkechaug Village of Poospatuck, the sole remainder of one hundred seventy-five acres deeded to the Unkechaugs July 2nd, 1700 from Col. William Smith, has been stripped down to fifty-five acres.

But the affinity of the people to the land is as strong as in the past, if not stronger today.

Today only two Long Island Indian Reservations remain, Poospatuck and Shinnecock, both in Suffolk County.

"Some Passed Poospatuck"

Chief, Sachems

Wyandanch: Grand Sachem of all Long Island

Weneco-heage "Wyongonheat" "Wiangonhut": – 1657
Tobaccus: 1664-1690
John Mayhew: 1691
Stephen Cuffee (Chief Cuffee):
Elizabeth Cuffee Job:

– 1832 Dormant –

Richard Ward: 1899
Jacob Ward: 1909
Fred Edwards:
Horace Wards: 1930
Walter J. Shepeard; Ceremonial Chief: 1950
Walter C. Treadwell: 1954
Edward Treadwell: 1957
Howard Treadwell:
Donald E. Treadwell: 1991

Presiding Chief: Harry B. Wallace: 1994

CHAPTER FORTY-NINE

"Great Grandma Line" Waters

My Great Grandmother, Adeline Waters was born in the year 1887. She a daughter of Solomon Waters and wife of Archibald Davis.

Archibald and Adeline resided in a second story apartment next to the railroad tracks on Little Neck Parkway in Little Neck.

Archibald, like his Father, William Davis, was a Sanitation worker for a private company.

Together Archibald and Adeline had four children. Charles, Solomon (Billy), Little Archie and Serena, my Grandmother.

Their youngest son, Archie Jr. suffered a fatal accident. While attempting to cross Northern Blvd. to catch up with his brothers, Charlie and Billy, he was struck down by a sanitation truck.

His tragic death at the age of five was the very first one to have occurred on Northern Blvd. in Little Neck. My Great Grandparents buried their son in the year 1915.

The loss of their child was just too much to bear. My Great Grandfather could not handle the death of his youngest son, and it ended his marriage with Adeline. Adeline Waters Davis, a Montaukett tribal member, died in the year 1933, of a ruptured appendix.

Archibald Davis suffered from drinking and haunted with many sadden memories was hospitalized in 1947 and sadly passed away in the year 1954.

CHAPTER FIFTY

"Serena Adeline Davis Barron" My Grandmother

Serena Adeline Davis was the youngest child of Archibald and Adeline.

Serena, my Grandmother, was born in their second story apartment down by the railroad tracks in Little Neck on March 12th, 1912.

She grew up in Little Neck. This is where she met my Grandfather, Nathaniel Corse Barron. They married in the year 1935.

Nathaniel was the son of James Nathaniel Barron and Elmira Corse. James emigrated to the U.S. in the late 19th century from British Guyana. Elmira was a Shinnecock Indian.

For, Elmira was the Granddaughter of Margaret Johnson, of the Shinnecock Reservation, Southampton, Long Island.

James worked as a Caretaker for the Van Vliet family of Douglaston. Clinton Van Vliet was an executive with Good Year Tire and Rubber Company. The Van Vliets constructed their large three story timber, stucco and stone house with wrap around porches and a castellated turret, set back on Main Ave. near the Douglaston Train Station. (Today it is the site of Public School 98 and the Community Church of Douglaston).

James was responsible for repairs and upkeep of the house, stable, and garage. He groomed the horse and later, cared for the family's 1912 Mitchel six cylinder, seven passenger automobile. He also did all the gardening and assisted the cook with shopping and errands.

He was given a small salary and the use of a large bedroom with a fireplace on the third floor under the turret.

After ten years with the Van Vliets, James married Elmira.

James gave up his lodgings and set up house with my Great Grandmother, in a Caretaker's cottage on the grounds of Zion Church in Douglaston. He continued to work for the Van Vliet family.

Clinton Van Vliet passed away in 1914. His Wife, Anna Elizabeth Van Vliet passed away in the following year, 1915.

James now no longer employed by the Van Vliets became a Chef at "Calter's Inn" and then was self employed as a Landscaper for many, many families in Douglaston, until his death on October 23rd, 1939.

Nathaniel was one of ten children of James and Elmira, raised in the Caretaker's cottage on the grounds of Zion's Church-yard.

My Grandparents, Nathaniel and Serena separated some six years after their marriage.

Serena went for training and became a Nurses Aide for Flushing Hospital. She also worked as a Domestic Helper.

My Grandmother worked long, grueling hours, for she was now a single parent, working hard to raise and support her three children on her own.

My Father James, my Aunt Nathalie, (Nagi) and my Uncle, Barry Barron.

Serena suddenly passed away in the year 1951 at the early age of just thirty-nine.

My Grandmother, Serena Adeline Davis Barron was interred alongside her family members an ancestors upon the very spot in which my Grandfather once lived.

On the grounds of Zion's Church-yard Cemetery in Douglaston, NY.

After her death, my Father, Aunt and Uncle went to live with their Great Aunt, Serena "Rene" Waters Barney. (Their Grandmother's sister).

They grew up in one of the last two original Waters' homesteads. The house their Great Grandfather, Solomon Waters built in the year 1901.

Until this day, they still reside upon the Waters family's homestead property. In the very house they were raised in. Their Great Grandfather, Solomon Jefferies Waters' home.

They, just like their Great Grandfather, cling to their Matinecock, Montaukett, and Shinnecock Native Roots.

I, myself today, am still learning, researching and exploring my Native background.

Most of Indian History with the various Long Island tribes has been passed down orally from generation to generation.

So in keeping with Indian tradition;

"Words cannot get lost"

I must thank my cousin LaRocque and his Grandfather, Chief John "Standing" Waters, for keeping with the Indian Tradition.

May Manto (God) bless you all

And may the Ancestors be

Smiling down upon my writings

And your reading.

Selected Bibliography

Vanessa Patterson, Southold Free Library, Historian,
Whitaker Collection 2/13/2004
"History of Eaton's Neck" by Mary Voyse 1955 www.Eatonsneck.org.

Quashawam Sunksquaw of the Montauk, the Long Island Historical Journal V3N2. Page 189-204. Written by Lara Strong & Selcuk Karabag.

"Shinnecock Indians" by Lois Marie Hunter publish 1950.
Tribal History- Pedigree of Uncas- 1) Colony Records, Deeds +c., iii, 312

The New England Historical and Genealogical Register July 1856
Http://www.nativeamericanmohegans.com/pedigree.htm
2) History of the Indians of Connecticut from Earliest Known Period to 1850. By John W. Deforest pgs.66-67 Hartford 1853.
Http://www.nativeamericanmohegans.com/pedigree.htm

"Wampum Archives" – www.History.digtalzones.com

History of Norwich Connecticut: From it possession by the Indians to the year 1866, by Frances Manwaring Caulking, 1866 page 30.
The Indian in his wigwam characteristics of the Red Race of America; from original notes and manuscripts by Henry R. Schoolcraft 1848.
Sachems of the Narragansett by Howard M. Chapin, 1931 by Providence Rhode Island Historical Society. A Son of the Forest by William Apes 1830 Ch.20 part 2.
Corchaugs Indians of Fort Corchaugs by Bob Liepa
Http://www.timesreview.com

"The Montaukett Indians of Eastern Long Island"
John Strong. "Poniute, alias Mousup: Wyandanch's Grandson"

www.longIslandgenealogy.com
"History of East Hampton, NY" "Chapter 7"
"The Indians": Wyandanch's Grandson, Moushu alias Poniute-signed the deed of Dec.1st, 1670.
Page 201. Quashawam: Sunksquaw of Montauk
Poniute, Montauk Sachem, signed a declaration of loyalty to Gov. Thomas Lovelace.
Poniute adopted the name Wyandanch after his Grandfather.
"Long Island History Journal "Quashawam: Sunksquaw of Montauk".
"The Montaukett Indians of Eastern Long Island"
Aquash "Aquaas" Young Sachem.
Mousup in 1684, it appears was preparing his son Aquash to assume authority over Montaukett affairs.

www.dominy.com/genealogy/newtonbook/chap1
Deed, Dec.1st, 1670; Sachem Mousup

www.longIslandgenealogy.com
Chap.7
History of East, New York chapter 7
"Wyandanch's Grandson; Moushu alias Poniute, signed the deed of Dec.1st, 1670.
www.mtsinai.com
"Colonial families settled on these lands and established farms. Farming was the main occupation. The lands brought from the Native Americans and divided up by the Colonialists."
"Shifted from hunting, fishing, farming habitat that sustained the Native population to a transplanted European population that farmed to sustain themselves and ship farm and forest products to cities to the north and west.

A History of the Episcopal Church in Narragansett Rhode Island. By; Wilkins Updike
Boston printed & published by D.B. Updike
The Merrymount Press 1907.
Pages; 8, 9, 10, 11 / chapter X pages; 252, 253

www.MaryARoots'homepage7
"Narragansett's"
Native American: The Tribes of Rhode Island
"Indians of R.I. Discovery of Estuarine Environments.

www.snowowl.com/peoplepequot
"Native American People/Tribes
"The Pequot"- The Destroyers
Pequot War: The History
Pequot History

www.our-oxford.info/other-history/indian.htm
Miantonomo's speech to the Long island Indians

www.simonpure.com/uncas03.htm
"The Mark of Uncas 3"

Daily Eagle Sunday February 16th, 1889
John Waters of Little Neck, Long Island.

"A Noted Long Island Indian and his Reminiscences." Flushing Evening Journal; Saturday February 5th, 1927
"Journal Discovers an Ancient Deed that may upset fight over Indian Cemetery Invasion"

Queens Borough Public Library: Long Island Collection
89-11 Jamaica, NY

Long Island Collection: The Queens Borough Public Library Jamaica, NY
1932; "Description of Private and Family Cemeteries in the Borough of Queens" Chap. 12. Page 43.
Zion Church Little Neck Parish Registers
1830- 1901/ 1901-1920/ 1920- 1936/ 1936

Shelter Island Historical Society
Manhanset Chapel Museum Exhibit; A
"Leap Back in Time"

East Hampton Library
East Hampton, NY 11937
"The PennyPacker L.I. Collection"

Alexandria Library
"Special Collections"
Alexandria, VA 22314
"Little Neck Then and Now"
By: Loys Gubernick 1991

Shinnecock History Sketch,
By; Harriet Crippen Brown Gumbs:
Encyclopedia of North American Indians 1990

"The Algonquin dialect of the Eastern Long Island Tribes"
James E. "Wati" Waters; Family Newspaper Article.

"Family Records"

Waters Family Deed 1902

Waters Family Deed 1949

"Marriage Records" / "Records of Death"
The City of New York Office of City Clerk
Borough Hall, NY
Bureau of Records
"Record of Marriage"

Dept. of Health of the City of NY
"Death Certificate"
Department of Health Vital Records
"Death Certificate"
"Birth Certificate"

Department of Veteran Affairs
Long Island National Cemetery
Farmingdale, NY

Brookhaven Census Records
1840, 1850, 1865.
Brookhaven Town (South) Long Island p.25
Town of Brookhaven 1800 Census

Medical Certificate of Death
Mastic, Long Island, NY 1933

Zion Church, Douglaston, NY
Certificate of Marriage
Baptismal Records /Burial Records

State of New York Certificate and Record of Birth
Metropolitan Hospital Morgue
1st Ave. & Twenty-Ninth Street
Manhattan, NY 10/30/1926

City of New York Dept. Public Welfare
Metropolitan Hospital
Welfare Island
Death Notice 1926

Funeral Directors;
Thomas Quinn & Sons, Flushing, NY
Joseph Mahood, Flushing, NY
Howard Hewlett, Flushing, NY
Lloyd Funeral Home, Bayside, NY
Shaffer Funeral Home, Douglaston, NY

Bayshore Southside Hospital
Suffolk County; Death Certificate 1951

Unites States of America Military Service
National Personnel Records Center.

U.S. Social Security Act.
Applications for Accounts.

Town Clerk/ Registrar
Records of Marriage / Transcript of Death
North Hempstead
220 Plandome Road
Manhasset, NY.

The Council of Seven/ Royal House of Pokanoket
Pokanoket Tribe / Wampanoag Nation

Bristol, R.I. 02809
Mr. Paul "Deerfoot" Weeden

Matinecock Long House
33-39 Union Street
Flushing, NY 11354
Chairman: Princess Sun Tama
November 13th, 1968

"Family Newspaper Articles & Stories"

North Shore Daily Journal
October 26th, 1932
"50 Indians Heirs Entitled to City Cemetery Award"
North Shore Daily Journal

September 15th, 1931
"Indians Bodies are moved in Little Neck"
N.Y.S. Long Island- Antiq.
Queens County

"Bayside Times" July 10th, 1949
"Old Indian Burial Plot with Colorful History Now is the Site of Stores".

North Shore Daily Journal
November 11th, 1931
"Indian Cemetery Dedicated"

Brooklyn Daily Star
October 16th, 1932
"Death Notice: Belinda Waters"

Long Island Daily Star
Tuesday February 17th, 1942
"Wigwam of Narraganset Princess"

The New York Times
1936, September 28th
"Matinecock Memorial Dedicated on Indian Plot"
Little Neck Ledger
Thursday November 26th, 1992
"Little Neck Indians Remember"
By; Robert Lothian

Flushing Evening Journal
Feb. 5th, 1927
"Deed May Upset Fight Over Indian Cemetery Invasion"

New York Times
"L.I. Indian Tribe asks Courts to settle Feud"
7/30/1983

"Move to 'Get Rid of the Indian's' is seen in States
Refusal to aid Mastic School"
New York Times
5/7/1935

"The Poospatuck Indians"
Story of an Almost Unknown Long Island Tribe
Life on the Reservation
The Brooklyn Daily Eagle; Sunday November 24th, 1895

Special to the Brooklyn Daily Eagle: June 12th, 1906
"June Meeting at Old Poospatuck"
Remnants of Long Island's Aborigines, met as usual

Long Island Advance; Thursday, December 5th, 1903
"Footnotes to L.I. History"
The Poospatuck Indians
By; Thomas R. Bayles
June 14th, 1909
"Poospatucks Meet"
"Gather Again in Memory of Dead Braves"
237th Annual Reunion Shows Falling off of Living
Members of Long Island Tribe

"Martha Mayne of Poospatuck Tribe, Dies at 98"
Special to the Herald Tribune
Mastic, Long Island July 7th, 1933

"Old Hampton Bays" Southampton Press
August 21st, 1976

"The Shinnecock Canal" L.I. Forum
Edward F. Pyle, October, 1939

The East Hampton Star August 6th, 1998
"What's in A Name?"
MASSACRE VALLEY

"Authors"

"Indians are Powwowing on Long Island Again"
The History and Archaeology of the Montauk
(Stony Brook, NY; Suffolk County Archaeological Assoc)
1993. Gaynell Stone.

Gaynell Stone; "The Shinnecock Indians: A Culture History" 1983

John Strong; "American Indian Culture and Research Journal 16 "Who Says the Montauk Tribe is Extinct.

John Strong; "We Are Still Here" 1998

John Strong; "The Montaukett Indians of Eastern
Long Island" 2001
"Sachem Wyandanch"

Nathan Cuffee; "Lords of the Soil"

Alvin G. Weeks; "Massasoit" 1920
"The Narragansetts"

Lara M. Strong; "Quashwam; Sunksquaw of the Montauk"
Long Island Historical Journal 1991

Lewis G. Knapp; "In Pursuit of Paradise"
History of the Town of Stratford, CT.

William Howard Wilcoxson: Historian
"History of Stratford Connecticut" 1639-1969
"Rev. Cuffee, Indian Preacher"
By; Thomas R. Bayles 10/30/1949

"Echoes from the Past"
The Legacy of Paul Cuffee, Indian Preacher
By; Elisabeth S. Lapham

"On the Poospatuck Reservation"
By; Helen E. Huntington

Early History;
Illustrated History of the Moriches Bat Area
(Excerpts)
By: Van and Mary Field

Brookhaven (Setauket)
Peter Ross
A History of Long Island; from its earliest settlement to the present time.
New York: Lewis Pub. Co. 1902

"History of Poospatuck Reservation"
By; Juanita Langhorn Mayo 1958

"My People, the Unkechaug"
The Story of a Long Island Indian Tribe
By: Chief Lone Otter Donald E. Treadwell

Excerpts from: "Isles of Shells" Long Island
By; George L. Weeks 1965

"Sketches of Suffolk County", Friedman, Port Washington 1873 Richard M. Bayles 1962

"The Early History of Southampton. L.I., N.Y". 2nd ed.
Yankee Peddler, Book Company, Southampton, N.Y. 1887 George R. Howell

Reading in L.I. Archaeology and Enthnohistory, vol 1 1977
Mark R. Harrington

"Indian Place Names; on L.I. and islands Adjacent"
William W. Tooker 1911
(Ira Freidman) Port Washington, NY reprint 1962

"Sketches From Local History" Yankee Peddler Book Co.
William D. Halsey Southampton, NY 1966

"History of Suffolk County, NY" 1683-1882
W.M. Munsell and Co., NY

"The First Book of Records of the Town of Southampton"
John Hunt Books, Sag Harbor, NY 1924

"Records of the deeds of Southampton" vol 1,
John Hunt Books, Sag Harbor, NY 1915

"REFERENCES"

Shelter Island Historical Society
"Corchaug" "Momoweta"
www.Shelterislandhistsoc.org
Records of the United Colonies of New England
(Which was a defense confederation consisting of CT., Mass. Bay, and Plymouth
Boston, September 19th, 1663
George Denison, John Stanton, Cary Latham
www.connhistory.org
"Sassacus' brother, Sacowawen"
"Tausaquonawhut son of Sassacus married Ninigret's daughter in 1649"
"Sachems of the Narragansetts" By: Howard M. Chapin
Sachem Sassacus' sister had five sons. They lived in a place called Soudahque. The five brothers grew so great and so proud that upon hunting they quarreled with the Pequot at which the Great Pequot Sachem being angry with them, made war upon them and conquered them. They all fled into Narragansett Country.
"Pedigree of Uncas.

Montaukett Tribal Rolls: 1922.

Long Island History: Southampton Village

www.nativeamericanmohegans

"New England Indians"
Chapter ten, Part two:
"One daughter of the Great Sassacus married Sausamon, a Ponkapoag, and they were both later adopted as Wampanoag "Some say that a daughter of Sassacus fled to the Montauks of Long Island. She married a Montauk Chief".

www.newigwam.com/wwwboard/genealogy/messages
From the book; "Sachems of the Narragansetts"
"Ninigret certainly had two daughters. One whom was married in 1649 to "Tausaquonawhut" son of Tatobem, Pequot Sachem and the other was married in 1650 to the son of the brother of Sassacus.
By; Howard M. Chapin
Long Island Historical Journal
"Quashawam Sunksquaw of Montauk"
Page 189- 203

"The land in what is now Smithtown had belonged to Wyandanch's Grandmother, who passed it along to him.
Long Island Antiquities
Page 58, 59, Page 60, 61

Topographical Bureau of the Borough of Queens W.P.A. project.
Flushing Evening Journal: February 5th, 1927
"Waters property Deed"

www.home.eznet.net/~dminor/nyny1660
"February 11th, 1663; the proprietors of East Hampton and Southampton approve the selection of Quashawam (Heather Flower) as Chief of the Montauk and Shinnecock Tribes".

Letter written by: Chief James Wild Pigeon Waters
Re: "The Indian Cemetery on Broadway, East of Cornell Lane, Little Neck, NY. Dated: December 2nd, 1919

Dictionary of American Fighting Ships
www.hazegray.org/danfs/steamers/uncas
"A Mohegan Chief, the son of Owenoco was born in or near 1588. In 1626, he married the daughter of Sassacus, Chief of the Pequots."

Terri Jean; the National Day of Mourning
A Different 'Thanksgiving' Perspective

Bryan Mitchell; www.su.ed/emuseum/cultural/northamerican/narragansett

Jennifer Bussian; www.su.ed/emuseum.cultral/northamerican/pequottribe

"Cruising Guide to Historic Rhode Island"
Published by; the Marine Advisory Service,
A Sea Grant Program, the University of Rhode Island, 1976.
Mashantucket Pequot Museum and Research Center"Cultural Differences between Natives and Europeans.
www.sachemfootball.com
"The thirteen tribes of Long Island"

www.buoy.com/setauket/setauket
Setauket Long Island, New York

www.hamptonbaysonline.com/history.php
PART III
INDIANS: Before Settlement

PART VII
SHINNECOCK CANAL

Legend tells us of a Shinnecock Chief Mongotucksee who Dug a ditch connecting the North and South Bays before the coming of the white man. By the time white men came there was no trace of there ever being such a canal but the need for one was seen as early as the 1600's. In the memorandum from an agent of Lord Sterling in 1640, Canoe Place is called a neck of land where the "Indians draw over their canoes out of north bay over to the south side of the island." This gives support of the argument that no water connected the two bays in early times.

www.longislandgenealogy.com/morichesarea

www.brookhaven.org

www.richmondhillhistory.orgindians

www.powertolearn.com/i_history/namer.html

www.bristolharborinn.com
"Chief, Sachem Massasoit"

Matinecock Tribe: March 8th, 1958 9:00 PM
Tribal Minutes
Ann H. Murdock
33-16 Prince Street
Flushing, NY
"Agenda"
Re: Organization of the Matinecock Tribe.

"13 Tribes Inhabited Long Island"
By; Thomas R, Bayles 4/22/1954

www.Runningdeerslonghouse.com
"The 13 tribes of Long Island
"Indian Land Bought"
"Town's early Settlers Lived peacefully with the Indians"
"The Poospatuck Tribe of Mastic"

Oyster Bay Historical Society
Oyster Bay, NY 11771

V.D.H.
Virginia Department of Health
Richmond VA, 23218-1000
West Virginia Div. of Culture & History
Charleston, W.V. 25305-0300

Office of the City Clerk
Central Falls, R.I. 02828

Rhode Island Genealogical Society
Greenville, R.I. 02828

Rhode Island Historical Society Library
Providence, R.I. 02906-2098

Scituate Historical Society
Scituate, Ma. 02066

Newport Historical Society
Newport, R.I. 02840

The New York Genealogical & Biographical Society
New York, N.Y. 10022-1939

George Hail Museum
Warren, R.I. 02885

Portsmouth Historical Society
Portsmouth, R.I. 02871

Town of Barnstable Office of Town Clerk
Hyannis, MA 02601
Linda E. Hutchenrider

Maryland Historical Society
Bristol Historical Society
Bristol, R.I.

Suffolk County Archaeological Assoc.
Nassau County Archaeological Committee
Stony Brook, NY 11790

Virginia Historical Society
Richmond, VA 23221-0311

Stratford Town Clerk's Office
Stratford CT. 06615-5892

Stratford Historical Society
Stratford CT. 06615-0382

Michelle Schimeel; Town Clerk
Manhasset, NY 11030

Miller Place-Mount Sinai Historical Society
Miller Place, NY 11764

City Hall; Dept. of the Board of Canvassers &
Registration
Pawtucket, R.I. 02860-2191

Office of the Town Clerk
Town of Southold
Southold, NY 11971

Rocky Point Historical Society
Rocky Point, NY

Martha Offerman; Town Clerk
Town of Oyster Bay
Oyster Bay, NY 11771-1302

Inc. Village of Lloyd Harbor
Huntington, NY 11743

Town Clerk of East Hampton
East Hampton, NY 11937

Village of Greenport
Janet E. Staples; Deputy Registrar
Greenport, NY 11944

Library Springs History Society
East Hampton, NY 11937

Lake Ronkonkoma Historical Society
Lake Ronkonkoma, NY 11779

The Smithtown Library
Smithtown, NY 11787-2143

Inc. Village of Roslyn
Roslyn, NY 11576-2127

New England Historic Genealogical Society
Boston, MA 02116-3007

Stratford Probate Court
Stratford, CT 06615

Connecticut State Library
Hartford, CT 06106-1537

Fairfield Probate Court
Sullivan Independence Hall
Fairfield, CT. 06430
Office of the City Clerk
City Hall
East Providence, R.I. 02914-4505

Town of Glocester
Town Clerk's Office
Clepachet, R.I. 02814-0702

Town of Charlestown
Charlestown,R.I. 02813

Town of West Warwick
Town Clerk's Office
West Warwick, R.I. 02893-4829

The Connecticut Historical Society
Hartford, CT 06105-2292

Massasoit Historical Society
Warren, R.I. 02885

Office of the Town Clerk
Lincoln, R.I. 02863

Town Clerk
Portsmouth, R.I. 02871

Office of the Town Clerk
Jamestown, R.I. 02835

Town Clerk's Office
Hopkinton, R.I. 02833-0038

www.narragansett-tribe.org/history

"In 1675, the Narragansett allied themselves with King Philip and the Wampanoag Sachem, to support the Wampanoag Tribe's efforts to reclaim land in Massachusetts. This war was the last major effort by the Indians of Southern New England to drive out the English settlers who wanted more Indian land.

But the Narragansett were completely defeated. For, a military force of Puritans from Plymouth, Massachusetts Bay, and Connecticut declared war. The United Colonies of New England raised a brigade of one thousand men and sent them to attack the Narragansett at the Great Swamp in West Kingston.

On a bitter cold December 19th, 1675 the troops marched and came upon a fortress containing six hundred lodges.

"The soldiers poured into the Narragansett's fort. The vengeful colonists massacred about six hundred Braves, women, children and Elders. They were burned to death in their lodges.

The fighting became hand to hand. Gradually, the Narragansett gave ground and were defeated. A few escaped deep into the forest and swamp lands.

Many who refused to be subjected to the authority of The United Colonies left the area or were hunted down and killed. Some were sold into slavery in the Caribbean, others migrated to Upstate New York and many went to Brothertown, Wisconsin.

After the war, the remaining Narragansett were forced to live on reservation lands.

Due to the increase in number of Colonists, the Narragansett hunting and farming grounds were greatly depleted. Colonists also introduced the common hog to the area. These domesticated hogs would roar along the coast and dig up the clam beds, a traditional food source for the Indians.

The tribe was under great pressure to abandon the traditional ways and adopt Waumpeshau (white man) ideas of civilization. As a result of dealing with the Waumpeshau, many debts were incurred which paid off by land grants. In 1790, the U.S. Congress introduced and passed the Non-Intercourse Act, which prohibited the taking of Indian lands as payment for debts incurred."

"During the 18th century, reservation life was extremely harsh. The State abolished the position of the Sachem, the traditional tribal leader, and took over the affairs of the tribe with a five-man council in 1792. However, tribal members continued to recognize the Sachems and traditional leadership.

By the end of the 18th century, the reservation, which is located near Charleston, Rhode Island had been reduced to 15,000 acres.

The Narragansett leaders resisted attempts by outsiders to take their remaining 15,000 acres of their reservation lands.

Then the State of Rhode Island illegally "detribalized" the Narragansett Tribe without federal sanction during the period of 1880-1884.

Even with the "detribalization" the Narragansetts continued to maintain their tribal customs and traditions and in the year 1901, there continued to be several leaders who were recognized both by the community and by outsiders as Narragansett tribal leaders.

In December of 1934 the Narragansett tribe of Indians was incorporated. The public once again recognized the offices of the Chief Sachem, Medicine Man, a nine-member Council, and Scribe and the office of the Prophet were re-established."

"Then in the early 1940s the Narragansett Indians built their Longhouse which became the center of tribal activities.

In the year 1974, the tribe filed a land claim suit against the State of Rhode Island and several landowners for the return of approximately 3,200 acres of undeveloped Reservation lands

Their suit eventually concluded in an out-of-court settlement in 1978 of approximately 1,800 acres.

A fifteen-volume petition for Federal Recognition was submitted to the Department of the Interior, Bureau of Indian Affairs in 1979.

Then at long last, on April 11th, 1983 the Narragansett Indian Tribe received federal recognition and acknowledgement!

It took decades but their persistence at getting back a part of what belonged to them finally paid off.

Here is where their heritage would live forever."

www.americaslibrary.gov/cgi-bin/page/es/ri/tribe_1

www.Montauklighthouse.com

www.onmontauk.com

www.oysterbayhistory.com

www.rootsweb.com

www.familysearch.com

www.ancestry.com

www.yahoo.com

www.google.com

www.Genealogy.com

www.vinlandsite.com

www.snowowl.com/peoplepequot

www.nativenewsonline.org/history

About The Author

Donna Barron born and raised in Flushing, Queens, began her red journey in 1994. Bringing her to a distant past filled with culture and history.

This quest has taught Donna about tradition held dear to her people and in November of 1999 she went through a Naming Ceremony and hence forth is known by those in the Native Community as Gentle Spirit.

Donna "Gentle Spirit" Barron continues to keep the history of her people, their Nation, from the Long Island Tribes alive.

Made in the USA
Middletown, DE
10 June 2024

55537372R00104